GEORGE MÜLLER

Man of Faith

Bonnie Harvey

BARBOUR
PUBLISHING, INC.
Uhrichsville, Ohio

Other books in the Heroes of the Faith series:

John Bunyan
William Carey
Fanny Crosby
Jim Elliot
Billy Graham
C. S. Lewis
David Livingstone
Martin Luther
D. L. Moody
Samuel Morris
John Newton
Charles Spurgeon
Corrie ten Boom
Mother Teresa
Sojourner Truth
John Wesley

©MCMXCVIII by Barbour Publishing, Inc.

ISBN 1-57748-177-1

Published by Barbour Publishing, Inc.
P.O. Box 719
Uhrichsville, Ohio 44683
http://www.barbourbooks.com

Member of the
Evangelical Christian
Publishers Association

Printed in the United States of America.

GEORGE MÜLLER

To Gary and Neil

Whose ancestors also came from Prussia—
May you always be blessed.

—

introduction

When someone asked George Müller if he had always found the Lord faithful to His promises, Müller did not hesitate, "Always. For nearly seventy years every need in connection with this work has been supplied." Müller was responsible for the care of thousands of orphans in Bristol, England, and amazingly, he never asked another person for help. He relied on God alone to supply his needs.

Talking with a friend, Müller emphasized his dependence on God for help: "During all these years I have been enabled to trust in God, in the living God, and in Him alone. We have needed as much as fifty thousand pounds in one year, and it has all come by the time it has been really needed. No man on earth can say that I have ever asked him for a penny. All has come in answer to believing prayer."

George Müller's remarkable life demonstrates that God answers the prayer of faith. From the time he became a Christian, Müller decided he would tell his needs to God alone—and to no one else. He believed God would prove

Himself faithful and trustworthy.

Nothing in George's background gave any indication of his becoming an outstanding man of faith. His family was not religious and knew little, if anything, of the Christian faith. George wasted his youth in a loose, dishonest, and even immoral lifestyle. Yet God had much in store for him, and when God entered his life, Müller became utterly transformed.

What credentials did George Müller have that prepared him for this life of faith? Was he someone special that God used to illustrate principles of prayer? How did he learn to trust God in such a remarkable way? What does the Bible mean by the "prayer of faith"? Do the passages in the Old and New Testaments that refer to this kind of prayer have meaning for us today?

Christians still consider these questions. Many wonder, too, whether the promises of God are available to them. In answer to these questions, the life of George Müller, an ordinary person without an exceptional background, provides positive answers and encouragement. If God could respond to George Müller's prayers the way He did, will He not also respond to ours?

one

George Müller's life began in Kroppenstaedt, Prussia (what is now Germany), on September 27, 1805. Little is known of the first five years of George's life, but in 1810, his family moved several miles to Heimersleben, where his father collected the excise, a form of tax placed on business houses and individuals for certain privileges. For the next eleven years, until George needed to prepare for the university, the family remained at Heimersleben.

"My father," George recalled later, "educated his children on worldly principles and gave us much money, considering our age. The result was that it led my brother and me into many sins. Before I was ten years old, I repeatedly took of the government money which was entrusted to my father till one day, he detected my theft. He had deposited a counted sum in the room where I was and left me by myself for awhile. I took some of the money and hid it under my foot in my shoe."

George's father was not to be fooled, for he soon discovered the loss, and on searching George, found the money.

But despite his father's punishment, George continued to deceive and cheat his father at every turn. He thought his sin was not so much stealing the money as it was getting caught! Before George was ten years old, he regularly practiced lying, stealing, and cheating.

George's thoughts reveal his attitude at this time: "Though I was punished on this and other occasions, yet I did not remember that at any time it made any other impression upon me than to make me think how I might do the thing the next time more cleverly."

Desiring his son to become a Lutheran minister, George's father sent him to the cathedral classical school at Halberstadt when he was eleven to prepare for the university. It didn't matter to George that he was training for a religious profession. Certainly Mr. Müller knew only too well George's moral deficiencies, but maybe George's father thought his son would be reformed as he studied.

George's father didn't understand what made a true Christian believer. He merely wished for his son to be in a profession that provided a comfortable living for him. In Prussia, the church and state were united, so a person working for the church also worked for the government.

At the age of fourteen, a tragedy occurred in George's life. His mother lay ill and dying. Instead of staying home, grieving with his family, George spent the night playing cards with some of his wild friends. His mother's death made little impression on him, and the following day, a Sunday, found George in a tavern, drinking with his friends.

On Mondays, George received his first religious instruction before being confirmed as a member of the church. But even this special instruction meant little to him. He was flippant and careless. Three or four days before his confirmation, which would allow him to partake of the Lord's Supper, he committed a horrible sin and saw no need to repent.

He had become so deceitful that he even lied to the minister who confirmed him: "I handed over to him only the twelfth part of the fee which my father had given me for him," George remembered.

He added: "In this state of heart, without prayer, without repentance, without faith, without knowledge of the plan of salvation, I was confirmed, and took the Lord's Supper, on the Sunday after Easter 1820. Yet I was not without some feeling. I made resolutions to turn from those vices in which I was living and to study more. But as I had no regard for God, and attempted the thing in my own strength, all soon came to nothing, and I still grew worse."

When his father was transferred to Schoenebeck by his company the next year, George asked his father if he could go to the nearby cathedral school at Magdeburg. Inwardly, George wanted to leave his sinful companions and have a fresh start. But the summer before attending school, George's father left him in charge of superintending some renovations on their house. George also studied the classics that summer with Dr. Nagel, a local minister. George collected the money owed to his father and spent it with his less desirable friends.

Then in November 1821, George gathered all the money he could find and left for Magdeburg. He spent six days at an expensive hotel and squandered his money living in what he later called "much sin." Taking whatever money he could gather through devious methods, he moved on to Brunswick and stayed a week at an expensive hotel there. When his money was gone, he tried to use the same tricks at a smaller hotel in a nearby village. But the hotel manager suspected he had no money and demanded that he leave his best clothes for security.

Sixteen-year-old George set out for Wolfenbuttel, a town six miles away, and attempted to repeat his escapades at a local inn. He acted as though he had plenty of money. But he got caught as he tried to escape from a high window. He finally admitted what he had done, expecting to be let off as he had in the past, but George was surprised to find his good fortune had fled.

He was arrested at once, taken to the police station, and jailed as a thief and vagabond. Of those dark days, George recalled, "I now found myself, at the age of sixteen, an inmate of the same dwelling with thieves and murderers, and treated accordingly. On the second day I asked the keeper for a Bible, not to consider its blessed contents, but to pass away the time." He remained in prison for twenty-four days—from December 18 to January 12. At that time, his father secured his release by paying the inn debt and his prison maintenance costs. He also provided enough money for George to come home.

In October of the next year, George entered school at Nordhausen and remained there for two and a half years while diligently studying Latin classics, French history, German literature, Hebrew, Greek, and mathematics. Of those days, he wrote, "I used to rise regularly at four, winter and summer, and generally studied all the day, with little exception, till ten at night." Because of his seriousness, his teachers held

George up as a model to the other students.

In spite of outward appearances, George admitted, "I did not care in the least about God, but lived secretly in much sin, in consequence of which I was taken ill, and for thirteen weeks confined to my room. During my illness I had no real sorrow of heart. I cared nothing about the Word of God. I had about three hundred books of my own, but no Bible." He added, "I practically set a higher value upon the writings of Horace and Cicero, Voltaire and Moliere, than upon the volume of inspiration." His student life centered around the typical university fare of the day rather than on anything pertaining to God and the Christian life.

Occasionally, George's conscience would bother him and he would resolve to be better, "particularly when I went to the Lord's Supper. The day previous to attending that ordinance I used to refrain from certain things; and on the day itself I was serious. But after one or two days were over, all was forgotten, and I was as bad as ever."

So George spent his youth squandering the money from his father in sinful pleasures. He quickly began to forge what he later called "a whole chain of lies." Once, when he had spent all his money, George resorted to a slightly different ruse. He pretended that his money had been stolen, broke the lock on his trunk and guitar case, and half-dressed, went into the director's room, telling him the story of the supposed theft. Incredibly, the story seemed to be true, and the director and others believed him. George mustered a certain amount of sympathy afterward.

At the age of twenty, with his excellent grades and references, George became a member of the University of Halle.

In turn, he was granted the privilege of preaching in the Lutheran Church. He began seriously to consider whether any church would have him as their pastor unless he reformed. Just as his father, George thought of the ministry as a means of earning a living, not as any service to the Lord or as a divine calling.

"I thought," he wrote, "no parish would choose me as their pastor and without a considerable knowledge of divinity I should never get a good living. But the moment I entered Halle all my resolutions came to nothing. I renewed my profligate life afresh, though now a student of divinity. I had no sorrow of heart on account of offending God."

In this frame of mind, but knowing he needed to improve, George met Christian student by the name of Beta. George thought: "It now appeared well to me to choose him as my friend, thinking that, if I could but have better companions, I should by that means improve my own conduct."

Both men guessed incorrectly about each other! On his part, Beta was a backslidden Christian who thought that friendship with George would bring him some of the worldly pleasures he sought. George thought Beta the perfect companion to help him on the way to self-improvement.

God was at work, however, in bringing the two unlikely individuals together, for it was through Beta that George would finally come to a saving knowledge of Christ. Concerning that time, he wrote, "My foolish heart was again deceived. Yet God in His abundant mercy made [Beta] the instrument of doing me good, not merely for time, but for eternity."

George admitted as well that after becoming friends with

Beta, his "conduct was outwardly better." But this improvement occurred not because of religious reasons but because he lacked money. Then, in August 1825, George and Beta and some other students, borrowed sufficient money on their belongings to travel through Prussia for a few days. Following this trip, they had a great desire to see the wonders of nature in Switzerland.

As usual, George and his friends needed money for their trip. But George's ingenuity soon produced the necessary money. Each student borrowed against his books and possessions. When they had enough money, they forged sufficient letters and papers to obtain their passports.

George later admitted that on this trip, he even deceived his companions: "I was on this journey like Judas. For having the common purse, I was a thief. I managed so that the journey cost me but two-thirds of what it cost my friends."

After forty-three days spent in traveling, the students returned to Prussia, and George stayed with his father the rest of his vacation. He determined again to change his lifestyle. But as he returned to the university with money in his pockets, his resolve crumbled.

In spite of his wayward behavior, George's life was about to change through a "chance" meeting. His friend Beta proved to be the instrument God would use to direct him. Someone has commented on George Müller's life up to this point: "The divine Hand [in his life] is doubly plain when we see that this was also the period of preparation for his life-work. During the next ten years we shall watch the divine Potter, to Whom George Müller was a chosen vessel for service, moulding and fitting the vessel for His use.

Every step is one of preparation."

Looking back, George, too, saw God's hand in his life: "The time was now come when God would have mercy upon me. At a time when I was as careless about Him as ever, He sent His Spirit into my heart. I had no Bible and had not read one for years. I went to church but seldom, but from custom, I took the Lord's Supper twice a year. I had never heard the gospel preached. I had never met with a person who told me that he meant, by the help of God, to live according to the Holy Scriptures. In short, I had not the least idea that there were any persons really different from myself."

Very soon, George's life would be changed forever as he left his sinful, wasted youth and life far behind and entered into a new life.

two

"I'm going to attend a cottage meeting on Saturday night. Would you like to come with me?" Beta asked George one mid-November afternoon in 1825 as they strolled along in an open field.

"I'm not sure. What do they do at these meetings?" responded George curiously.

Beta replied: "Well, they read the Bible, sing a few hymns, pray, and someone reads a printed sermon."

Beta's telling me this makes me think as if I have found something which I have been seeking all my life long, George thought.

He said later, "We went together in the evening. As I did not know the manners of believers, and the joy they had in seeing poor sinners caring about the things of God, I made an apology for coming."

But Mr. Wagner, a Christian tradesman in whose house the meeting took place, reassured George with a grin: "Come as often as you please; house and heart are open to you!"

After everyone had been greeted and made to feel

comfortable, Mr. Wagner led the group in singing a hymn. Then a man by the name of Kayser—who later became a missionary to Africa under the London Missionary Society—opened the meeting with prayer. As everyone knelt in prayer, Kayser beseeched God to work through the meeting.

"I had never either seen anyone on his knees, nor had I ever myself prayed on my knees," George confessed. Until that time, his life had been one with little prayer in it. He had not yet learned the wonder that comes from asking God for life's blessings. Seeing Kayser on his knees worked a change in the entire course of George's life. He found at last the things for which he had sought.

The prayer over, Kayser read a chapter from the Bible and a printed sermon, since it was not legal for a layman to preach his own sermon in Prussia. After singing a final hymn, all the believers again knelt down while Wagner led the concluding prayer.

George thought as he listened to the tradesman's eloquent pleas, *I could not pray as well, though I am much more learned than this illiterate man.*

For the first time in his life, George felt truly happy. "If I had been asked why I was happy, I could not have clearly explained it," he noted much later.

As they walked home, George told his friend Beta, "All we have seen on our journey to Switzerland, and all our former pleasures, are as nothing in comparison with this evening."

Upon reaching his home, George knelt to pray. A deep, settled peace came over him. When it was time to sleep, he recalled, "I lay peaceful and happy in my bed."

God had begun a work of grace in George Müller's heart. He now had a deep sense of joy that sprung up with scarcely any sorrow in spite of his little understanding and knowledge. Looking back several years later, George marked that night at Wagner's home as the night of his conversion to Christ. And the path God led him on would grow continually brighter as his understanding increased.

His life changed forever, George now read the Scriptures eagerly instead of the classics. He prayed often and attended church when prompted by the Lord. Even at the university, when his fellow students taunted him for taking on the cause of Christ, he did not go back to his old ways.

By January 1826, George considered becoming a missionary. He had met Hermann Ball, a learned and wealthy young man who worked as a missionary in Poland among Jewish people. But his missionary efforts at that time consisted mainly of writing family members and entreating them to "seek the Lord" so they could be as happy as he was. His father responded angrily in a letter urging George to "stop all this nonsense" and get to work making out of himself an accepted minister—a clergyman with a good living, who would be able to support his father in his old age.

About this time a well-known theology professor, Dr. Tholuck, came to teach divinity at the university. This godly man drew students to him, and from him, George grew stronger in his faith. George realized that he could be independent of man only by being more entirely dependent on God, and that henceforth he should take no more money from his father. To receive such support implied obedience to his father's wishes, for it seemed plainly wrong to expect his father to cover the cost of his training when George had no intention of meeting his father's expectations. So early in his Christian life, George Müller began to learn the valuable lesson that he must preserve his independence if he did not want to endanger his integrity.

Before long, God supplied George's financial needs. Dr. Tholuck recommended George to a group of American professors who needed someone to teach them German. George marveled at the time, "Thus did the Lord richly make up to me the little which I had relinquished for His sake."

Though he was a ministerial student, George had not yet preached. When the opportunity came, he agonized through his sermon, for he tried to preach in his own strength. A teacher had arranged for him to speak in the parish of an older minister, and on August 27, 1826, George went out and spoke at the morning service, having written and memorized his message. However, the message brought no unusual blessing from the Lord.

In the afternoon George had another service at which he was allowed to speak more freely than in the morning. "It came to my mind to read the fifth chapter of Matthew, and to make such remarks as I was able. Immediately upon beginning to expound 'Blessed are the poor in spirit,' I felt myself greatly assisted; and whereas in the morning my sermon had not been simple enough for the people to understand it, I now was listened to with the greatest attention. My own peace and joy were great."

This experience launched George on a preaching career, which from then on led him to a simple exposition of the

Scriptures. He continued to use this method and never deviated from it the rest of his life.

A common error George succumbed to as a divinity student was reading books about the Bible instead of reading the Bible itself. George admitted, "I practically preferred for the first four years of my Christian life the works of uninspired men. The consequence was that I remained a babe, both in knowledge and grace."

Though George attended church regularly when not preaching himself, the ministers he heard were often unenlightened spiritually, and there was little in their sermons to feed his soul. As a result, he rarely heard the truth, and would walk ten or fifteen miles to hear a godly minister expound the Word of God.

Each week he faithfully attended the meeting at Johann Wagner's house—the place where he had found Christ—and these meetings remained the one bright spot in the week. On Sundays he also went to a meeting of religious students, which grew from six to twenty while he was at Halle.

Another significant step George took at this time brought him into contact with orphanage work and later proved to be the model for his own orphanages. For two months George lived in free housing furnished for divinity students in the famous Orphan Houses built by A. H. Francke. More than a hundred years earlier, Francke had been led to establish an orphanage, depending entirely upon God for the success of the work. Francke died in 1727, but by faith the work continued. Francke's work and dependence upon God became an inspiration to George, and he often recorded how much he was indebted to the example of trust and prayer which Francke showed.

In August 1827, when George was twenty-two, he learned that the Continental Society in England planned to send a missionary to Bucharest to assist a long-term missionary in his work. After much prayer, George offered himself to Dr. Tholuck, who had been asked to help find the right candidate for the work.

Even though George's father unexpectedly "gave his consent" following much prayer on George's part, God intervened. The war between the Turks and the Russians caused the society to abandon the idea. George knew then that God had something else in mind for him.

He persisted in prayer as he sought God's will for his life. While George strongly sensed the call and the challenge to become a missionary, the Lord never permitted him to serve in this capacity. God had other plans for George Müller's life.

George had become interested in Hebrew at this time and studied hard to master the difficult language. Calling upon Dr. Tholuck on November 17, George mentioned his interest in Hebrew. Dr. Tholuck asked, "Would you like to serve as a missionary to the Jews?" The professor went on to say that he was connected with the London Missionary Society for Promoting Christianity among the Jews.

George was about to experience a miracle in his life— one that would have far-reaching results not only for him but for many others as well. Sometimes God chooses to lead an individual indirectly to his field of service. This was the case with George. God wanted him to be in England, where his future sphere of influence would be centered.

When Dr. Tholuck learned of George's interest in Jewish missionary work, he quickly wrote the London Society suggesting his name as a candidate. The society answered the following March, asking the candidate a number of questions, and on June 13, 1828, a letter came saying they would take George as a missionary student for six months on probation. The one requirement they insisted upon: He must come to London.

George still faced a seemingly insurmountable obstacle. Every Prussian man had to serve three years in the army, but classical students who had passed the university examinations only needed to serve one year. Since George had not yet served in the army, he could not receive a passport to leave the country. He became quite depressed when his application for exemption was denied. But God had already made other plans to use it.

In Leipsic a short time later, George attended an opera with an American professor he was tutoring. During intermission, George had some refreshments that made him ill and then ruptured a blood vessel in his stomach. His friends advised him to go to Berlin for advice from medical experts about his condition. While he was there, George not only got the medical help he needed, but he found an open door to preach in the poorhouse and in the prisons.

On February 3, 1829, he was re-examined for the army, and because of his stomach trouble, declared physically unfit for service and exempted. Quickly, George received his passport and set sail for London. He arrived on March 19.

While waiting for his missionary appointment in London, George learned of a dentist, a Mr. Groves, who refused a salary of $7, 500 a year to be a missionary to Persia, simply trusting in God to meet his material needs. "This made such an impression on me," George stressed, "that I not only marked it down in my journal, but also wrote about it to my German friends."

The hand of the Lord was evident once more in George's life, leading him into a life of trust. But at this time, his stomach trouble flared up again, and for weeks he despaired of life itself. "I longed exceedingly to depart and be with Christ," he recalled.

"Oh Lord," he prayed while on his sick bed, "do with me as seemeth best." The Lord answered his prayer in time, but very slowly. He permitted his servant to languish in sickness so his soul might learn a new lesson in trust.

A short time later George went to Tiegnmouth to recuperate. As it turned out, Ebenezer Chapel had been reopened, and he had the privilege of living for ten days with the preacher. During this brief stay, "God began to show me," George said, "that His Word alone is our standard of judgment; that it can be explained only by the Holy Spirit; and that in our day, as well as in former times, He is the teacher of the people."

These few days might have seemed meaningless to George, but he realized later that he had learned an invaluable lesson about the Bible. For the Bible became, from then on, the true source of his inspiration, and the one book to which he was solely devoted.

He began an experiment. He would test the Bible's truth by experience: "The Lord enabled me to put it to the test of experience, by laying aside commentaries, and almost every other book, and simply reading the Word of God and studying it. The result of this was that the first evening I shut myself into my room to give myself to prayer and meditation over the Scriptures, I learned more in a few hours than I had done during a period of several months previously. . . . But the particular difference was that I received real strength for my soul in doing so."

God used George's brief sojourn in the country to bring about a great change in his understanding of the Scriptures. From then on, through meditation upon the Bible and prayer, George committed his ways to the Lord. Near the end of his life he said he had read the Bible through approximately two hundred times, one hundred of them on his knees. He found God's promises in the Bible and experienced the truth of them in his daily life. He learned to believe what he read and to act accordingly. He mined religious truth, not from books of human fabrication, but from God's Word—and what George read, he lived.

The time had come for George to be sent to his mission field as a full-fledged apostle of trust. Yet he still had one more lesson to learn before God could use him to the fullest: He had to learn to tell God, not man, his needs and to believe God would supply them. Through circumstances, God was about to teach George this necessary lesson of trust.

three

I n his new zeal, George felt impatient to serve God on the mission field, but more mature believers advised him to wait for divine guidance until he took further steps. George thought to himself: *I just can't wait any longer! I know what I'll do—what they did in the Old Testament. I'll cast lots! In fact, I'll enter the Royal Lottery, and if I win a prize, I'll take that as a sign to go to the field. If not, I won't go.*

When the lottery ticket won a small amount of money, he immediately applied to the Berlin Missionary Society. Because George lacked his father's consent, however, the society refused his application.

Certainly this episode again displayed God's hand in George's life. The Lord had overruled in George's decision, and now George would have to wait until God made a way for him to serve. Someone has said that George needed to learn "that primary lesson that he who would work with God must first wait on Him and wait for Him, and that all undue haste in such a matter is worse than waste." After all, God kept Moses waiting forty years before He sent him to lead

Israel from Egypt's bondage; He sent Saul of Tarsus (later the apostle Paul) into Arabia for three years before sending him forth to preach to the Gentiles; and even Jesus lived in obscurity for thirty years prior to His final three years of ministry.

George still had not learned this basic lesson of waiting, and he resorted to "casting lots" two more times: once at a literal parting of the ways when the lot led him to take the wrong fork in the road, and later in a far more important decision, but with a similar result. Both times, he realized he had been misled. Then and there, George determined: *Never again will I resort to such carnal methods of finding God's will for my life. I will steel myself to wait as long as it takes to obtain His answer for me. That way, I will be certain of His leading and guidance in my life.*

He did learn two valuable lessons from his "lot casting" experiences: First, that the safe guide in every crisis is believing prayer in connection with the Word of God; and second, that continued uncertainty about one's course is a reason for continued waiting.

Much later George realized the utmost importance of these two basic lessons, and he confided to a friend the difficulty in achieving both: "The flesh is impatient in all delay, both in decision and action—hence, all carnal choices are immature and premature, and all carnal courses are mistaken and unspiritual. God often delays that we may be led to pray, and even the answers to prayer are deferred that the natural and carnal spirit may be kept in check and self-will may bow before the will of God."

Reviewing his life in later years, George saw, too, that he had "run hastily to the lot as a faster way of settling a

27

doubtful matter," and that especially regarding such an important decision as to God's call to the mission field, this method was totally undesirable. What he understood afterward as well was his lack of readiness to go to the mission field. How could he who was "so ignorant and needing to be taught himself even think of teaching others"! He could not teach others the most elementary gospel truths. What he needed early in his Christian life was to gain "a deeper knowledge and a deeper experience of divine things" through much prayer and Bible study.

Still experiencing episodes of his stomach sickness, George spent some time recuperating in the countryside of Devonshire. The rest did him good and strengthened not only his body but his spirit as well. He had prayed at the outset of his time there that God would bless the journey to the benefit of body and soul. Following this time, he noted, "In the beginning of September [1829] I returned to London, much better in body, and as to my soul, the change was so great that it was like a second conversion."

Back in London, George desired to do something for the Lord, so he started a prayer meeting for the seminary students, having them meet for devotions from six to eight every morning. Following these sessions he would often be so caught up with joy that he remained in an attitude of prayer long after the others had left. In the evening, too, after family devotions, George would continue praying until midnight, then awake in the morning and begin again with the students at the six o'clock meeting.

In his enthusiasm, George contacted the London Society about appointing him to work with the Jews in that area.

But after some time when he still had not received an answer, he began his own work. He distributed tracts, taught a Sunday school class of about fifty Jewish boys, and read the Bible to them.

While he waited for men to send him out into God's work, George began to believe it was wrong to wait for an appointment. He should receive orders from the Holy Spirit even as Paul and Barnabas did in the book of Acts. During Christmas vacation with friends in Devon, he wrote the Society expressing his views. Then he told them: "I'll gladly work without any salary if you will let me go wherever the Lord directs me."

At the same time, he began to look to God instead of men to give him spiritual direction as well as to provide for his physical needs. This was a new step toward a life of total trust. Before God could use him, George needed to learn this lesson well. When he first came to England as a total stranger, he knew that he didn't need to worry: "As long as I sought the kingdom of God and His righteousness, these my temporal wants would be added unto me."

As George studied the Bible and thought about its promises, they came alive to him. In turn, George saw the divine supply provided in these "precious promises" of whatever was needed. He didn't need to ask men to provide for him; his God could and would supply his needs. As George came to this conclusion, certain verses spoke to him:

Ask, and it shall be given you; seek and ye shall find; knock, and it shall be opened unto you."

Matthew 7:7

*And whatsoever ye shall ask in my name, that will
I do, that the Father may be glorified in the Son. If
ye shall ask any thing in my name, I will do it*
                                            John 14:13-14

*Therefore I say unto you, Take no thought for your
life, what ye shall eat, or what ye shall drink: nor
yet for your body, what ye shall put on. Is not the
life more than meat, and the body than raiment:
Behold the fowls of the air: for they sow not, neither do they reap. . .yet your heavenly Father
feedeth them. Are ye not much better than they?*
                                            Matthew 6:25-26

The more George thought about and meditated on verses
such as these, the more his faith surged forth. Either God
meant what He said in the Bible, or He didn't! The Lord
Himself seemed to be beckoning George to come close to
Him and receive all He had to give—whatever the need.

In January 1830, the society sent word to George that
his relationship with them had ended. Although the door
was closed for George to be a missionary to the Jews, God
seemed to be opening another door. At age twenty-five,
George felt exhilarated as he looked upon the whole world
as a field of service. He was willing for the Spirit to guide
him and provide for him.

After receiving the society's news, George stayed on in
the south of Devon and preached wherever he had the opportunity. Then he preached at Ebenezer Chapel and spoke on
the difference between a Christian and a happy Christian,

"and showed [the congregation] whence it generally comes that we rejoice so little in the Lord."

He brought the afternoon message as well, and when he finished, he was asked to begin a series of morning messages on the Book of Romans. During the time of these messages, the Ebenezer Congregation asked George to be their pastor. However, they were not unanimous in their choice. George knew that "some of them left and never returned; some left, but returned after a while; others came to the chapel who had not been in the habit of attending previous to my coming."

Some of the congregation were troubled because George was not English. But others rejoiced in receiving food for their souls—they little cared what package the food came in! Still others bitterly opposed the work of Christ. George recalled: "There was in addition to this, a great stir, a spirit of enquiry, and a searching of the Scriptures. And what is more than all, God set His seal upon the work in converting sinners. Twelve weeks I stood in this position, whilst the Lord graciously supplied my temporal wants, through two brethren, unasked for."

After the series concluded, the Ebenezer Church, eighteen in number, asked George to become their permanent pastor. In their generosity, they gave the offered salary of 55 pounds, or $275 a year (an English pound represented approximately five dollars).

Although his desire had been to travel and preach the gospel, George waited for the Lord's answer to the call he had received. During this time of waiting, he also came to a new understanding of baptism. When preaching at Sidmouth in April, three ladies wanted to know his opinion on baptism.

"I do not think that I need to be baptized again," he told them.

One of the ladies asked, "But have you been baptized?"

"Yes, when I was a child," was his response.

"Have you ever read the Scriptures and prayed with reference to the subject?" another queried.

George confessed he had not.

One of the women brought him up short by saying, "Then, I beg of you not to speak any more about the subject until you have done so."

George felt humbled by those remarks. He thought, *Why, I never really gave baptism much thought—the Lord never brought it to my attention—but I believe He wants to show me about it now.*

As he diligently searched the Scriptures, especially passages such as Acts 8:36-38 and Romans 6:3-6, George said, "I saw that believers only are the proper subjects for baptism, and that immersion is the only true Scriptural mode in which it ought to be attended to." Not long after coming to this conclusion about baptism, George was baptized by immersion himself.

four

N ot long after his decision to be baptized, George searched the Scriptures to see what they said about the Lord's Supper. Finishing his search, he thought it seemed scriptural "according to the example of the Apostles (Acts 20:7) to break bread every Lord's day, though there is no commandment given to do so either by the Lord, or by the Holy Ghost through the apostles." George also came to believe as he studied Ephesians 4 and Romans 12 that people should be given an opportunity to speak freely in their meetings—whether they wished to testify, exhort, or teach—as the Holy Spirit led them.

God seemed to be leading George into an ever-deeper level of trust, and now He wanted George to trust the Scriptures for guidance in matters of conscience. George had begun trusting the Scriptures and yielding in minor things, so the next step of trusting God for all his supplies did not seem too difficult. A short time later, George made up his mind to trust the Lord totally for every need.

At this time George decided to take another extremely

important step. He would trust God to bring him a wife! He prayed and searched the Scriptures earnestly, reminding the Lord of verses such as:

Whoso findeth a wife findeth a good thing, and obtaineth favour of the Lord.

Proverbs 18:22

House and riches are the inheritance of fathers: and a prudent wife is from the Lord.

Proverbs 19:14

Very shortly, George found a "prudent wife" and delighted in the choice: "On October 7, 1830, I was united in marriage to Miss Mary Groves. This step was taken after much prayer and from a full conviction that it was better for me to be married. I have never regretted either the step itself or the choice, but I am truly grateful to God for giving me such a wife," exulted George.

Someone observed about the Müllers: "Married life often has its period of estrangement, even when temporary alienation yields to a deeper love, as the parties become more truly wedded by the assimilation of their inmost being to one another. But to Mr. and Mrs. Müller there never came any such experience of even temporary alienation. From the first, love grew, and with it mutual confidence and trust." So close was their union, in fact, that Mary stayed in total agreement with her husband when it came to matters of trusting the Lord.

About the time of his marriage, George became concerned about the thought of a stated salary. He believed that he should trust God to provide for him. He thought of three reasons why he should not accept a fixed salary:

1. A salary implies a fixed sum, generally made up of pew rents. According to James 2:1-6, however, "Pew rents are against the mind of the Lord because the poor brethren cannot afford as good a seat as the rich."

2. A fixed pew rent may occasionally become a burden to the follower of Christ, especially when he has other expenses and of necessity has to contribute to a salary, "I do not know whether he pays his money grudgingly or cheerfully, and God loves a cheerful giver." George did not want to lay the tiniest obstacle in the way of the church's spiritual progress.

3. The whole system of pew rents and salary can become a snare to the minister, in that he works for hire rather than for spiritual reasons. "Fear of offending those who pay his salary has kept many ministers from preaching the uncompromising Word of God," George reasoned.

Within a month after their marriage, George and Mary had talked the matter of a salary over and agreed that he should no longer accept one. Soon George told his congregation that he had decided not to receive a regular salary and trust the Lord to meet his needs. He asked that a box be placed in the chapel so that whoever desired to contribute might leave his offering. George added that from now on he would ask no one, "not even my beloved brethren and sisters, to help me; for unconsciously I had been led to trust in an arm of flesh, going to man instead of going to the Lord at once."

A short time later, George and his wife felt impressed by the Lord to take another step of faith. As they read the text, "Sell that ye have and give alms," they knew the Lord had spoken to them to do just that. George remarked, "Our staff and support in this matter were Matthew 6:19-34 and John 14:13-14. We leaned on the arm of the Lord Jesus." Always, however, the Müllers sensed the Lord's faithfulness to them.

They never looked back, nor did they regret following the Lord's leading in the matter of selling their earthly possessions. In spite of their willing obedience in disposing of their material things, the Müllers still underwent some strong testings. Yet they knew that if God fed, clothed, and housed the sparrows, He would do no less for them. The Lord wanted to teach them to walk by faith and not by sight. So they had to learn the lesson of trust by going through various experiences.

At first their trials were not too difficult. George noted, "He [God] did not try our faith much at the commencement, but gave us first encouragement, and allowed us to see His willingness to help us before He was pleased to try it more fully."

One morning when they had just eight shillings left— about two dollars (a shilling being equal to nearly twenty-five cents) —George went to the Lord for money. The Müllers waited about four hours and heard nothing. Then a lady came to their house.

"Do you want any money?" she asked.

His faith intact, George replied, "I told the brethren, dear sister, when I gave up my salary, that I would for the future tell the Lord only about my wants.

"But," she responded, reaching into her purse, "He has told me to give you some money," and placed two guineas in his hand. George noted, "Throughout 1830, the Lord richly supplied all my temporal needs, although I could not depend upon any human for a single shilling."

At the year's close, George reported ecstatically that the Lord had "richly supplied all our temporal wants, though at the commencement we had no certain human prospect of a single shilling, so that we have not been in the smallest degree a loser in acting according to the dictates of conscience. The Lord dealt bountifully with me, and has condescended to use me as an instrument in doing His work."

The next year, 1831, would be one of intense trial. Many times there was not a single shilling in the Müller home. Then at the right time, as the Müllers continued looking to God, their reward would arrive in the form of money and supplies.

God allowed the Müllers' faith to be strenuously tried on January 6, 7, and 8. All their money was gone. George prayed earnestly and faithfully, but still nothing came. The Müllers were tempted to distrust the Lord. Then George remembered God's faithfulness up to this time: "He had not only supplied all our needs but had given us many miraculous answers to prayer. I began to think it would be of no use to trust in the Lord this time. Perhaps I had gone too far in living by faith. But praise the Lord! This trial lasted only a few minutes. He enabled me to trust in Him, and Satan was immediately defeated."

Some ten minutes later when George returned to his room, the Lord sent deliverance. "A sister brought us two pounds, four shillings. The Lord triumphed, and our faith was strengthened."

Another time when the Müllers desperately needed money, George found himself getting anxious observing a brother open the chapel box. He dared not ask the man how much money had come in since he often mentioned in the pulpit, "I desire to look neither to man nor the box, but to the living God." Instead, George prayed: "Lord, incline the man's heart to bring me the money." Almost as soon as George prayed, the man brought him the money, which totaled one pound, eight shillings and sixpence.

Another test came on February 14. The Müllers had very little money, and George knelt to ask God to supply their needs. "The instant that I got up from my knees, a brother gave me one pound which had been taken out of the chapel box." The Lord used George's walk of faith to strengthen his fellow believers. Many times he encouraged his poorer brethren to trust the Lord for their needs even as he had learned to do.

In March, George was tempted again to doubt the faithfulness of the Lord. He said, "Although I was not worried about money, I was not fully resting upon Him so that I could triumph with joy. One hour later the Lord gave me another proof of His faithful love. A Christian lady brought five sovereigns for us, with these words written on paper: 'I was hungry and ye gave me meat; I was thirsty, and ye gave me drink.'"

A startling episode occurred on April 16 when the Müllers' money supply was reduced to three shillings. George told himself, *I must now go and ask the Lord earnestly for fresh supplies.* "But before I had prayed," he later wrote, "two pounds were sent from Exeter as proof that the Lord hears before we call."

Later that year the Müllers didn't have money to pay the rent. After George prayed, the money arrived. Following this incident, George set forth a principle which he tried to maintain from then on: "I would just observe that we never contract debts, which we believe to be unscriptural (according to Romans 13:8), and therefore we have no bills, but all we buy we pay for in ready money. Thus we always know how much we have and how much we have a right to give away." George applied this principle later on when he managed several orphanages. He never deviated from this rule of staying out of debt.

God continued to lead George in the way of complete trust. Frequently the Müllers would not even have bread for the next meal, but it would always arrive in plenty of time. George recalled one such incident: "Our bread was hardly enough for the day. After dinner, when I returned thanks, I asked Him to give us our daily bread, meaning literally that He would send us bread for the evening. While I was praying there was a knock at the door of the room. After I had concluded a poor sister came in and brought us some of her dinner, and from another poor sister five shillings. In the afternoon she also brought us a large loaf. Thus the Lord not only gave us bread but also money." In these ways, the Lord repeatedly proved His faithfulness to the Müllers.

George also believed that laying up stores or hoarding money was inconsistent with a life of faith. In such cases, he maintained, God would send them to their savings before answering their prayers. Experience confirmed their belief that a life of trust forbids laying up treasures against unforeseen needs, since with God "no emergency is unforeseen and no want unprovided for." So George looked to God for every need—and refused to fall back on "hoarded money."

George followed a third rule throughout his career of trust. When someone gave him money for a specific need or purpose, George regarded the money as sacred to that trust, and would not use or borrow it even temporarily for any other purpose. Even if he and his wife were reduced to desperate need, he would not use the money set aside for other purposes except for its original intent. Thousands of times came where temporarily using funds in an emergency would have made a way out for him or assisted them through a tight place, but he refused to use money that way.

George kept an accurate record of what the Lord sent him. At the end of his first year of trusting God to supply everything, he could honestly say, " Now the truth is whilst we have not had even as much as a single penny left, or so as to have the last bread on the table, and not as much money as was needed to buy another loaf, yet never have we had to sit down to a meal without our good Lord having provided nourishing food for us. I am bound to state this, and I do it with pleasure. If I had to choose this day again as to the way of living, the Lord giving me grace, I would not choose differently."

At the end of 1831 as George added up what he had received in answer to prayer it amounted to more than 131 pounds, three-fourths of which came from friends not connected with his church. The congregation had offered their minister $275, and through a life of trust he had received approximately $600 for the year.

George rejoiced in his new-found freedom of simply trusting God to take care of everything. He said, " In this my freedom, I am at least able to say to myself, my Lord is not limited; He can supply. And thus this way of living, so far from leading to anxiety, as regards possible future want, is rather the means of keeping from it. This way of living has often been the means of reviving the work of grace in my heart. . .and a fresh answer to prayer obtained in this way has been the means of quickening my soul and filling me with much joy."

five

Now George began to feel a restlessness within—a sense that the Lord had something new for him to do. For the past few years he had practiced living by faith, according to the teaching of Scripture. No longer did he look to people to meet his needs. He looked to God alone.

God had taken him from his birthplace in Prussia to England and had taught him many lessons in trust. The Lord had seen fit to remove everything and every person George could possibly lean on. He also looked to God alone in all other matters of spiritual direction, including that of bodily health.

At this time, George realized that the "work at Tiegnmouth [Ebenezer Chapel] is no longer my place of ministry. Perhaps my gift is going from place to place, seeking to bring believers back to the Scriptures, rather than staying in one place and laboring as a pastor. Wherever I go, I preach with much more enjoyment and power than at Tiegnmouth. And almost everywhere I have many more hearers than at Tiegnmouth and find the people hungering after spiritual food which is no longer the case at Tiegnmouth." So the promptings within George to go somewhere else continued, to reach new people for the Lord.

But where did God wish for him to go? God would not cause these inner stirrings and put new desires in him without showing him where to go. George needed a place to apply all the principles of trust he had learned. The Lord began to give him his answer in a rather unusual way.

George reported that on April 13, 1832, "I received a letter from Brother Craik from Bristol inviting me to come and help him. It appears to me that a place like Bristol would suit my gifts better. Lord, teach me! I feel more than ever that I will soon leave Tiegnmouth. But I fear that much connected with this decision is of the flesh. It seems to me that I will soon go to Bristol, if the Lord permits." The next day George responded to Brother Craik that he would be happy to come if he knew it to be the Lord's will.

Not one to act without the Lord's leading, George always waited for a definite indication from God before he would proceed. He made his decisions only when his plans and the Lord's coincided. Then he would have the Lord's peace according to Colossians 3:15: "And let the peace of God rule in your hearts, to the which also ye are called in one body; and be ye thankful." When the peace of God ruled in his heart, George knew the Lord had shown him which way to go.

Preaching at Tiegnmouth on April 15, George brought his congregation a message on the Lord's second coming. He shared with them the effect this doctrine had on him and how it encouraged him to leave London and to preach "throughout the land." The Lord had kept him at Tiegnmouth for two years and three months, and "it seemed that the time was near when I should leave," he said. He also reminded them of what he had told them when he first came to be their pastor: "That I could stay only as long as I saw it was the Lord's will to do so." The people wept much when George shared these things with them, but as he said later: "I am now again in peace."

After visiting Bristol on April 21, George preached at Gideon Chapel and later at Pithay Chapel, and decided it was God's will to leave his Tiegnmouth congregation. He and Mr. Craik were able to agree concerning the conditions for the new congregation to accept before they would become their pastors.

George received two letters from Bristol on May 15, in which the Gideon congregation accepted his terms as follows: "To consider us only as ministering among them, but not in any fixed pastoral relationship, so that we may preach as we consider it to be according to the mind of God, without reference to any rules among them; that the pew-rents should be done away with, and that we should go on, respecting the supply of our temporal wants, as in Devonshire."

The Müllers were partially packed when the letters arrived, so that within a ten-day period, they had moved to Bristol. George was at last in the place where God's plan for him would be fulfilled through his faith.

Prior to leaving the Tiegnmouth congregation, George needed to say his farewells. On May 21, he noted: "I began to say good-bye to the brethren at Tiegnmouth, calling on each of them. It has been a trying day, filled with much weeping. If I was not fully persuaded that God wants us to go to Bristol, I would have hardly been able to bear it." He realized that some of the people expected the Müllers to come back. But it was his conviction that they would not return other than for occasional visits.

Another confirmation for the Müllers in moving to Bristol came as they looked for the right place to live. Unable to find something simple and inexpensive, they "began to make this a matter of earnest prayer. Immediately afterward, the Lord gave us a suitable place. We wanted to find a furnished place with five rooms since brother Craik would be living with us. How good the Lord is to have answered our prayer, and what an encouragement to commit everything to Him in prayer!" Once more, George's faith took wings as he saw the Lord repeatedly answer his diligent prayers.

On the first Sunday that George preached at Pithay Chapel, several conversions resulted. A young man, a notorious drunkard, found faith in Christ as a result of the sermon, and the Lord's hand of blessing was much in evidence for the first nine days of meetings. During the last day of the services at Gideon Chapel, many people had to be turned away for lack of room. Brother Craik, of course, shared these services with George, and at that time, was the better known in the Bristol area.

As if to confirm that the Müllers were indeed in the right place for them, God opened another pulpit for George and Mr. Craik. With the opening of the Bethesda Chapel, each man had his own pulpit. From the first, God blessed the meetings greatly. In his writings, George mentioned that aside from the regular meeting times, an evening was set aside just for inquirers: "This evening from six to nine o'clock, we made appointments to talk with individuals about salvation. Many people prefer coming at an appointed time to the church office to converse with us. Appointing a time for counseling with them in private concerning the things of eternity has brought some who never would have called upon us under other circumstances."

He said, too, that these office appointments provided encouragement to the preachers and the personal workers: "Often when we thought that our teaching of the Word had done no good at all, we found the opposite was true as we counseled with people. We have been encouraged to go forward in the work of the Lord after seeing the many ways the Lord has used us as His instruments. Individuals have told us about the help they derived from our ministry even as long as four years ago." George admitted, though, that the appointments proved the most exhaustive part of their work.

An important meeting took place on August 13, 1832, between George, Mr. Craik, and five others: one man and four women. They sat down together, uniting in church fellowship "without any rules—desiring to act only as the Lord should be pleased to give light through His Word." The significance of this meeting lies in George's desire to build an apostolic church with no manual of guidance but the New Testament.

This meeting took place during an epidemic of cholera. The disease broke out in mid-July. This terrible "scourge of God" continued for three months. Prayer meetings were held often—and for a time daily—to plead for the removal of the dreaded disease. Mr. Craik and George visited the sick and risked their lives to care for the dying. George agonized, "Who may be next, God alone knows. I have never realized so much the nearness of death. Just now, ten in the evening, the funeral bell is ringing, and has been ringing the greater part of the evening. It rings almost all the day. Into Thine hands, O Lord, I commend myself." Despite their many visits to the sick and dying that summer, George and Mr. Craik remained healthy. Only one child died from cholera.

On September 17, in the midst of all this gloom and sorrow, a little daughter was born to George and Mary. They named her Lydia, and she became a great blessing not only to her parents, but also to everyone who knew her.

By October 1, George commenced a season of soul searching. He realized that "many more people have been convicted of sin through brother Craik's preaching than my own." He attributed these results to brother Craik's being more spiritually minded than himself. George also thought, "He prays more earnestly for the conversion of sinners than I do. He addresses sinners in his public ministry frequently. This led me to more earnest prayer for the conversion of sinners. Since then, the Lord has used me as an instrument of conversion much more often." The Lord used brother Craik to bring needed humility to George.

Throughout the terrible summer of cholera, the blessings of God were still evident in the two chapel groups. But on January 4, 1833, a disturbing ripple flowed through the congregations—they might lose their pastors! For both George and brother Craik received a letter that day from Baghdad inviting them to come there as missionaries. The letter even included a one-thousand-dollar draft to cover their traveling expenses. But as the men prayed and sought God about the matter, He made it apparent they should remain in Bristol because of His blessing on the work there.

The work in Bristol was so fruitful that George described the inquirers' meetings to be "so largely attended that, though they sometimes lasted for more than four hours, it was frequently the case that many had to be sent away for lack of time and strength on the part of the two workers." For eight years, Gideon and Bethesda Chapels were the scene of George and Mr. Craik's fruitful ministry.

At the close of 1833, George reviewed God's dealings with him since he had begun to live by faith alone in the promises of God. He discovered that his income for this time was approximately $3,700, whereas his stated salary for the same length of time would have been only about $900. "During the last three years," he declared in reviewing his income through faith, "I never have asked anyone for anything; but, by the help of the Lord, I have been enabled at all times to bring my wants to Him, and He graciously supplied them all."

Some of George's incentive to continue living by faith had come through a book on August H. Francke's life. George had received a copy of Francke's book the previous year. As he read its inspiring pages, he was greatly encouraged. For over thirty years of Francke's life, God had been able to supply all the needs for over two thousand orphans, and for well over one hundred years, Francke's work had been continued through faith. Francke was from the same part of Prussia as George. In about 1696 at Halle, Francke had begun the largest work that existed anywhere in the world for poor children. Francke trusted in God to provide for this work, and he was never disappointed in the Lord's provision.

George was also moved by the condition of the orphans

and homeless children on the streets of Bristol. Inspired by Francke's book, he decided to gather them together so he could instruct them from God's Word. Not only were the children poor, but "most of the Lord's people whom we know in Bristol are poor. This morning, while sitting in my room, the distress of several of the brethren was brought to my mind. I said to myself, If only the Lord would give me the means to help them! About an hour later, I received sixty pounds which I used to buy bread for the poor." The Lord had begun a new facet of George's work in Bristol.

At eight o'clock every morning, George invited the street children into his home, fed them breakfast, and then, for an hour and a half, taught them from the Scriptures. The work increased until it included older people as well. Soon he found himself feeding from thirty to forty people, and as the number increased, the Lord's provisions also increased. One kept pace with the other.

Sharing his burden with Mr. Craik, George soon located another place which could hold one hundred fifty children and which could be rented for ten shillings yearly. Several obstacles, however, prevented this plan from working. George and Mr. Craik already had their hands full with the rapid increase of applicants for food, and the neighbors expressed annoyance at the crowds of people gathering and being idle in the streets. So George abandoned this plan. But he did not lose sight of the desire to reach the children. Someone observed that "God had planted a seed in the soil of Mr. Müller's heart, presently to spring up in the orphan work." And George added, "This thought ultimately issued in the formation of the Scriptural Knowledge Institution and in the establishment of the Orphan Houses."

On January 9, 1834, George reported that "during these past eighteen months, brother Craik and I have preached once a month at Brislington, a village near Bristol. This led me to pray earnestly to the Lord for the conversion of sinners in that place. I asked the Lord to convert at least one soul this evening so that we might have a little encouragement. Tonight a young man was brought to the knowledge of the truth." So the Lord continued His faithfulness to George as he looked steadfastly to God to supply everything.

Doubtless February 21, 1834, was the crowning day up to that time of God's dealings with George Müller. "I was led this morning to form a plan for the establishing, upon Scriptural principles, of an institution for the spread of the gospel at home and abroad," George reported. "I trust this matter is of God." From then on, God filled nearly every waking moment of George's life with the idea of such an institution.

Several reasons prompted this action. Other societies, George realized, were based on the assumption that the world would gradually become better and better, "and at last the whole world will be converted." George believed this view was contrary to the Bible, and so he could not endorse it.

Neither did the worldly connection of these other societies line up with biblical teachings. As George noted: "The connection with the world is too marked in these religious societies, for every one who pays a guinea is considered a member and has a right to vote." Other societies also asked the unconverted for money. George opposed any such practice. The leaders in such societies were often wealthy, but unconverted, and so they had no true knowledge of God. The final reason George had for not believing in existing organizations lay in their "contracting debts." Long ago, the Lord had taught George not to go into debt; he believed that people who went into debt were not trusting God. "It appeared to us to be His will," George explained, "that we should be entirely separate from these societies."

So on the evening of March 5, 1834, a public meeting was held to form "The Scriptural Knowledge Institution for Home and Abroad." A statement of principles and objectives accompanied the announcement. These were the ten principles:

1. We consider every believer bound to help the cause of Christ.
2. We never intend to ask unconverted persons of rank or wealth to countenance this institution. In the name of God we set up our banners.
3. We do not mean to ask unbelievers for money.
4. We reject altogether the help of unbelievers in managing the affairs of the Institution.
5. We intend never to enlarge the field of labor by contracting debts, but in secret prayer, we shall carry the wants of the Institution to the Lord, and act according to the means that God shall give us.
6. We do not reckon the success of the Institution by the amount of money given but by the Lord's blessing upon the work.
7. We desire to go simply according to the Scripture, without compromising the truth.

8. We consider it unscriptural that any person who does not profess to know the Lord themselves should be allowed to give religious instruction. The Institution does not assist any adult school—the main difference between the two is that the teachers are believers.

9. To circulate the Holy Scriptures.

10. We desire to assist those missionaries whose proceedings appear to be most according to the Scriptures.

These goals were an ambitious undertaking for George, especially when he wrote two days later: "Today we have only one shilling left." That shilling needed to stretch between two preachers and their families. There were no patrons, no committees, and no membership. There was to be no asking for funds, and the responsibility rested solely upon the frail efforts of two ministers, both of whom were decidedly poor!

Even though the institution's regulations forbid looking to worldly means to support it, George's excitement over the Lord's leading could scarcely be contained. On the same day (March 7) that they were reduced to one shilling, George rejoiced over new clothes: "This evening when we came home from our work, we found our tailor waiting for us. He brought a new suit of clothes for brother Craik and me, which another brother had ordered for us." How faithful the Lord was to him!

Now that the principles of the Scriptural Knowledge Institution had been set forth, everything appeared to be in place for George to take the next step. God had been preparing him all along. By now, George had learned to look to God's Word and His promises to supply his daily needs, to provide direction and guidance, and to furnish strength for each day. God had found a man He could trust and was about to use him mightily in a new work.

six

George sensed a new stirring within. From his early days as a Christian, he had wanted to serve on the mission field, but God always seemed to close the door. After all these years, George had learned to take counsel and direction entirely from God. He had discovered the power for spiritual empowerment which lies in Bible reading and had filled his soul with God's Word so that he might test his daily walk by these God-inspired principles.

He discovered another source of spiritual strength by separating himself from worldly attachments. He determined not to give any money to a school or a Sunday school where the teachers were not believers, nor would he list wealthy patrons as promoters of his work—neither would he ask money from anyone. He had renounced self, the world, and its attachments that he might give himself to secret prayer. George's new ministry would flow from his power with God in prayer.

During the Institute's first seven months, money came in and several activities were begun. When a number of people gave 168 pounds, the money was carefully allocated to promote various projects. Some of these projects included: 120 children received instruction; 40 people were taught in the adults' school; 209 children were taught in the four day schools, two for boys and two for girls (54 of this number were free pupils, the others paid part of their expenses).

Bible distribution, one of the main objectives of the Institute, began immediately. The Institute distributed over 482 Bibles and 520 New Testaments in the first seven months. At the same time, it gave $285 to assist various missionary activities.

On January 21, 1835, George wrote: "I received, in answer to prayer, five pounds for the Scriptural Knowledge Institution. The Lord pours in, while we continue to pour out. During the past week, fifty-eight copies of the Scriptures were sold at reduced prices. We want to continue this important work, but we will require much financial help." The Lord always seemed to answer George's prayers with just the right amount: never too much, never too little!

George had struck a partnership with God and had promised to dispense whatever the Almighty provided. As he worked diligently to promote the Institute's goal of reaching the unconverted abroad as well as at home, George often felt a tug on his heart toward foreign missionary service. He wrote on January 28, "I have prayed much to ascertain whether the Lord will have me to go as a missionary to the East Indies, and I am most willing to go." The next day he added: "I have been greatly stirred up to pray about going to Calcutta as a missionary. May the Lord guide me in this matter." However, God did not choose to send George to the mission field. He had other plans for him that involved staying right in Bristol.

In later years George could see how God used his missionary zeal even though he never went to the mission field. He continued to pray earnestly for various mission fields around the world and sent funds as the Lord directed him. God used George's prayers mightily, carrying them forth on the streams of influence that emanated from Bristol, England —one of the world's busiest sea ports.

Throughout 1835, George's vision for the Institute of Scriptural Knowledge began to bear fruit. In February he noted: "In the name of the Lord and in dependence on Him alone for support, we have established a fifth day school for poor children, which opened today. We now have two boys' schools and three girls' schools." To himself, George mused: *Never in my wildest dreams could I ever have thought God would do such marvelous things in answer to prayer! I give Him all the praise and glory for what He chooses to accomplish through me.*

At a public meeting of the Institute in June, George gave a positive report of the Institute's activities for the past fifteen months. He said that they had been able to provide many poor children with schooling, to distribute Bibles, and to help in missionary activities. He added that "the number of children that have been provided with schooling in the day schools amounts to 439. The number of copies of the Holy Scriptures circulated is 795 and 753 New Testaments. We have also sent aid to missionary labors in Canada, the East Indies, and on the continent of Europe."

Yet during this time, George experienced some intense

personal struggles of his own. He wrote on June 25: "Our little boy is so ill that I have no hope of his recovery." Sadly, the next day George recorded: "My prayer last evening was that God would support my dear wife under the trial. Two hours later, the little one went home to be with the Lord. I fully realize that the dear infant is much better off with the Lord Jesus than with us, and when I weep, I weep for joy."

A few weeks following his child's death, George admitted to feeling a weakness in his chest for several days. With concern, he wrote: "Today I felt it more than ever, and think it would be wise to refrain next week from all public speaking. May the Lord grant that I may be brought nearer to Him through this." In a short time, God sent George and brother Craik (who also suffered from illness) a former minister to help them. George called his visit "a divine appointment" as this man "began to go from house to house to spread the truth as a city missionary." George and brother Craik both rejoiced over the Lord's provision through this minister to further their work.

George's health continued to plague him. He tried several home remedies but did not seem to get much better. On August 24, he complained: "I feel very weak and suffer more than ever from the disease. Should I leave Bristol for a while? I have no money to go away to recover. A sister in the country invited me to visit for a week, and I may accept the invitation and go tomorrow." As George committed his illness to the Lord, God began to make some provisions for him.

A short time later (on August 26), someone gave George five pounds specifically so he could take some time off. A few days after that, he received five more pounds for the same purpose! Then, on September 19, he received a letter from a family who lived on the Isle of Wight: "They invited me to come and stay with them for some time. They wrote that they had repeatedly prayed about the matter and were persuaded that I ought to come. The Lord graciously provided the money so that my family and I could travel there for the rest that we needed." George was so grateful to see that the Lord's care for him extended to arranging a much-needed rest for him.

George shared an insight concerning his illness on September 29: "Last evening when I said good night to the family, I wanted to go to sleep at once. The weakness in my body and the coldness of the night tempted me to pray no longer. However, the Lord helped me to kneel before Him. No sooner had I begun to pray than His Spirit shone into my soul and gave me such a spirit of prayer as I had not enjoyed for many weeks. He graciously revived His work in my heart. I enjoyed that nearness to God and fervency in prayer for more than an hour. My soul had been panting for many weeks for this sweet experience."

In addition, George recalled that "for the first time during this illness, I asked the Lord earnestly to restore me to health. I now long to go back to the work in Bristol, yet I am not impatient. The Lord will strengthen me to return to it. I went to bed especially happy and awoke this morning in great peace. For more than an hour, I had real communion with the Lord before breakfast. May He in mercy continue this state of heart to His most unworthy child!"

Between early October and mid-November, George and his family continued to visit the Isle of Wight and enjoyed a wonderful time of rest. George, in particular, savored this time not only to get away from his regular duties of preaching, teaching, and ministering, but to be able to bask in the Lord's presence in unbroken prayer and communion. He knew his strength came from these times, and it was difficult to maintain these unhindered times back in Bristol.

At last the time came for the Müller family to return to Bristol. In an evening devoted to prayer (November 15), George and several others "prayed repeatedly concerning the work of the Scriptural Knowledge Institution and especially that the Lord would give us the means to continue and even enlarge the work. I have also asked for my own needs to be met, and He has kindly granted both these requests. May I have grace to trust Him more and more!"

God had greater things in store for thirty-year-old George Müller. The Lord had taught George to trust Him completely for his every need and even restored him to health in response to prayer. George had already been occupied with reaching out and ministering to the homeless children on the streets of Bristol. Even though he ministered to many of these children, there were so many more that needed to be reached! The idea of ministering to more children—orphaned children—continued to develop in George's soul. And he waited, as always, for God's perfect timing to proceed.

seven

Through the Lord's leading, George had been made ready to fulfill his life's work. At Bristol, his soul had been strengthened by eighteen months of trust for the institution's success. Now God was ready to thrust him forth into his real mission. All the other activities were preparatory to the orphanage work. Through the circuitous paths of providence, God had prepared a man of faith to whom He could trust this important activity.

For a number of months, George had been thinking about founding an orphanage. He had prayed much about it, and his classes for destitute children and older folks gradually led him to the decision that God's time had finally arrived.

Picking up August Francke's book again on November 20, 1835, he thumbed through its pages. His heart leaped as he re-read of God's dealings with Francke and how God faithfully supplied every need for those orphanages. George reported: "I have frequently, for a long time, thought of laboring in a similar way. Today I have had it very much impressed on my heart no longer merely to think about the establishment of an orphan house, but actually to set about it. I have been very much in prayer regarding it. . .to ascertain the Lord's mind." By December, George planned to reveal his dream of an orphanage to his brethren.

George didn't have to wait for the brethren's opinion, advice, or any first-fruits of meager gifts. For on December 5 while reading the Bible at his evening prayer season, the Scriptures blazed forth in a text which inspired his faith to immediate action.

"This evening," he wrote, "I was struck in reading the Scriptures with these words, 'Open thy mouth wide, and I will fill it' [Psalm 81:10]. I was led to apply this Scripture to the orphan house, and ask the Lord for premises, one thousand pounds and suitable individuals to take care of the children." George's faith surged when God spoke to him.

From that time on, Psalm 81:10 formed one of his life's mottoes, and the promise became a power in shaping his future work. His check on heaven's bank, the text could be made cashable for any amount needed, as his faith testified. George was so excited! He prayed: *Lord, is it really possible that You will provide whatever I ask You for—especially concerning the orphan house? I praise You, Lord. Truly You are great and greatly to be praised that a mere man can ask of You, the God of the universe, and receive whatever he asks. Help me to be faithful to Your calling, Lord.*

George shivered as he thought of the great calling—and responsibility—God had for him.

As if to encourage George in his forthright praying, God soon sent in a monetary gift. Now George sensed his faith growing by leaps and bounds. He recorded in his diary:

"Today I received the first shilling for the orphan house. . . just two days after I asked the Lord for specific provisions for this work!"

On December 9, the scheduled meeting day, George's faith again took wings. Someone contributed a large wardrobe for storing clothes: the first gift of furniture! But something else occurred during the evening meeting. God put His stamp of approval on George and this new work. George exclaimed: "As soon as I began to speak at the meeting I received peculiar assistance from God. After the meeting ten shillings were given me. There was purposely no collection. . .After the meeting a sister offered herself for the work. I went home, happy in the Lord and full of confidence that the matter would come to pass."

The next morning the press received a statement of the meeting. Following the article's release, gifts began to pour in, and numerous people offered their services.

George received a typical letter on December 10, one of many throughout his long career directing the orphanages. The letter read: "We propose ourselves for the service of the intended orphan house, if you think us qualified for it; also to give up all the furniture, etc., which the Lord has given us, for its use; and to do this without receiving any salary whatever; believing that, if it be the will of the Lord to employ us, He will supply all our needs." From that time many other capable, godly workers appeared to help George in the work.

The evening of the same day brought in more gifts for the orphanage, as George meticulously recorded: "three dishes, twenty-eight plates, three basins, one jug, four mugs, three saltstands, one grater, four knives and five forks." Two days later, on December 12, George received more dishes and fifty pounds for the work. On December 13, twenty-nine yards of print were given, and "a sister offered herself for the work." Calm and serene in his disposition, George reported each gift equally. Of course he was pleased, but his pleasure came from the generosity of his God. As he witnessed God's hand moving so faithfully in his circumstances and in answer to prayer, George could do nothing but rejoice.

Other gifts trickled in—eight shillings, "a brother and sister offered themselves," basins, mugs, dessert spoons, a skimmer, a toasting fork, pillow cases, table cloths, a dredge, and "fifty-five yards of sheeting and twelve yards of calico" also came in. The orphanage was well on its way to becoming a reality. God was answering George's prayer: "Open thy mouth wide, and I will fill it."

On December 17 George turned down a gift of five hundred dollars from a poor seamstress, thinking that she could not afford to give so much. She earned only a few shillings a week from her work and was not strong physically. George wrote, however, "Before accepting the money, I had a long conversation with her. I needed to know her motives, and whether she might have given this money emotionally, without having counted the cost. But I had not conversed long with this beloved sister before I found that she was a quiet, calm, considerate follower of the Lord Jesus. She desired, in spite of what human reasoning might say, to act according to the words of our Lord, 'Lay not up for yourselves treasures upon earth' (Matthew 6:19); and 'Sell that ye have, and give alms' (Luke 12:33)."

The woman rejoiced to give the money. She told George triumphantly: "The Lord Jesus has given His last drop for me, and should I not give Him this hundred pounds?" He discovered later that the gift had come through the death of the woman's grandmother. Accepting the gift with gratitude to God, George realized that God had used "this poor, sickly sister as an instrument in so considerable gift, for helping at its very commencement the work."

In addition, George noticed four things about "this beloved sister":

1. She did all these things in secret and thus proved that she did not desire the praise of man.
2. She remained, as before, of an humble and lowly mind. She gave her money for the Lord and not to impress man.
3. During all the time that she had this comparative abundance, she did not change her lodging, dress, or manner of life. She remained in every way the poor handmaiden of the Lord to all outward appearance.
4. She continued to work at her sewing all this time, earning three shillings or a little more a week while she gave away the money in five-pound notes.

"At last all her money was gone several years before her death," George recorded. "She found herself completely dependent upon the Lord, who never forsook her, up to the last moments of her earthly life. Her body grew weaker, and she was able to work very little. But the Lord supplied her with all she needed, although she never asked for anything. For instance, a sister in our fellowship sent her all the bread she needed. She was full of thanksgiving, always praising the Lord." This gift and the way it came proved a great encouragement and blessing to George.

Finally George was able to set a definite date for opening an orphans' house for girls. As funds came in, he rented the large house where he had been living for some time—6 North Wilson Street—for a year. The formal opening date for the house was April 2, 1836.

On April 2, George wrote joyously: "This day was set apart for prayer and thanksgiving for the opening of the Orphan House. In the morning, several brethren prayed, and brother Craik spoke on the last verses of Psalm 20. I addressed our day and Sunday school children and the orphans; and in the evening, we had another prayer meeting." George had told the public earlier that he would receive applications for entrance, and shortly after he intimated that a second house would be opened to receive small children, both boys and girls.

But on opening day, George had a shock. For weeks, George had prayed in the materials for the house, the funds for the rent and its equipment, the laborers to carry on the work. But when the orphanage was ready for children, not one applicant had been received!

George had taken it for granted that the children would come. He spent two hours at the house waiting for applicants, and then dejectedly went for a walk. On his way this thought rushed to his mind, *I have prayed about everything connected with this work—for money, for a house, for helpers, about the various articles of furniture, etc., but I have never asked the Lord to send me orphans!*

That night George humbled himself in prayer, prevailing with God to send children for the home. His faith once more brought the Lord to his aid, and the next day he received the first application for entrance. Within a month forty-two children sought admission, with twenty-six already in the home and more arriving each day.

A short time later, George noted: "For several weeks our income has been low. Although I prayed many times that the Lord would enable us to pay our taxes, the prayer remained unanswered. The Lord will send help by the time it is needed." He added, "One thing particularly has been a trial to us lately, far more than our temporal circumstances. We have scarcely been able to relieve the poverty among the poor saints. Seven pounds twelve shillings were given to me as my part of the freewill offerings through the boxes, and two five-pound notes were put in yesterday—one for brother Craik and one for me. Thus the Lord has again delivered us and answered our prayers, not one single hour too late. The taxes are not yet due. May He fill my heart with gratitude for this fresh deliverance. May He enable me to trust more in him and to wait patiently for His help!"

George endured many tests of faith throughout the year, but God never failed him. He told of one such trial on November 30: "On account of many pressing engagements, I have not prayed about the funds for some time. But being in great need, I was led to earnestly seek the Lord. In answer to this petition, a brother gave me ten pounds. He had it in his heart for several months to give this sum, but had been kept from it, not having the means. Now, in our time of great need, the Lord furnished him with the means, he used it to help us."

George also received a letter with five pounds from a woman whom he had never met. She wrote: "It has been on my mind lately to send you some money, and I feel as if there must be some need. I therefore, send you five pounds, all I have in the house at this moment." These answers to prayer formed a pattern in George's life: he prayed, and the Lord sent back. He testified in his middle years that five thousand of his definite prayers had been answered on the day of asking.

Keeping a notebook of two-page entries became a daily habit for George. On one page, he wrote the petition and the date, and on the opposite page, he entered the date of the answer. By following this procedure, he was able to keep track of definite petitions and their specific answers. He advocated a similar method to believers who desired specific results to their prayers. Each believer could write down the petition and its date followed by the date of the Lord's answer. Such a method took the guesswork out of God's answers to prayer.

In January 1837, George had asked the Lord for a thousand pounds and an orphanage house along with its equipment. Reviewing that year's work, he discovered that not only had God given him the first orphanage house on Wilson Street (6 North), but He had also provided a second one seven months later at 1 Wilson Street. A review of his financial returns showed that gifts for the orphanages totaled

770 pounds, and he himself had received 232 pounds for his personal needs.

Throughout the year, God had furnished more than the five thousand dollars requested for the beginning of the work. At the close of the orphanages' first year, George Müller rejoiced in God's faithfulness: "On December 31, we had this evening a prayer meeting to praise the Lord for His goodness during the past year, and to ask Him for a continuance of His favors."

God had also abundantly answered George's prayers for children to live in the orphanages. By April 8, 1837, there were thirty orphans in each house. Older girls lived at 6 Wilson Street, while 1 Wilson Street housed younger boys and girls. So far, God had been pleased to answer George's prayers, but would He continue to answer every prayer so specifically?

George had such confidence and trust in the Lord that he counted his requests as good as accomplished when he prayed. He often thanked God for the sum as though already in hand. On May 28, 1837, George noted that "the narrative of some of the Lord's dealings with me is now ready to be published. I have asked the Lord to give me what is lacking of the one thousand pounds. In my own mind, the thing is as good as done, and I have repeatedly thanked God that He will surely give me every shilling of that sum. I earnestly desired that the book not leave the press until every shilling of that sum had been given in answer to prayer. Thus I might have the sweet privilege of bearing my testimony for God in this book."

On June 15, George recorded: "I again prayed earnestly for the remainder of the thousand pounds. This evening five pounds were given so that now the whole sum has been received. For the last eighteen months and ten days, I have brought this petition before God almost daily. From the moment I asked until the Lord granted it fully, I never doubted that He would give every shilling of that sum. Often I praised Him in the assurance that He would grant my request. When we pray, we must believe that we receive according to Mark 11:24, 'What things so ever ye desire, when ye pray, believe that ye receive them, and ye shall have them.'" In humility, George believed that God had given him "a special gift of faith in His promises."

Even so, in 1837, at the age of thirty-two, George was convinced that his own growth in grace and power for service were indispensable for the continuance of the orphanage work. He sought two things: first, more time for secret prayer and communion with God, and second, provision for the spiritual oversight of the church. Since the total number of parishioners had reached four hundred at this time, he found himself too busy to pray as he desired.

After learning the lesson of being busy in the work of the Lord, too busy in fact to pray, he told his brethren that four hours of work after an hour of prayer would accomplish more than five hours without prayer. George faithfully kept this rule the rest of his life. Then, another answer to his prayer came when the two separate congregations from the two churches expressed a desire to unite. Such a union decreased the number of meetings that had to be held each week.

On October 21, 1837, another house was opened on Wilson Street to house orphan boys. The total number of orphans under George's care now totaled ninety-six. In addition, his prayers for premises, suitable helpers, and the thousand pounds had been abundantly supplied. On such definite answers to prayer, George remarked: "When I was asking the petition I was fully aware what I was doing; i.e., asking for something that I had no natural prospect of getting from the brethren I knew, but which was not too much for the Lord to grant."

As he reviewed the year of 1837, George noted that eighty-one children lived in the three Orphan Houses, and nine workers cared for them. Then, he prayed: "Ninety people daily sit down to the table. Lord, look on the needs of Your servant! The schools require even more help than before, particularly the Sunday school in which there are about 320 children. Lord, Your servant is a poor man, but I have trusted in You and made my boast in You before the sons of men. Do not let me fail in this work! Let it not be said all this was mere emotion and enthusiasm and will eventually come to nothing!" To God's glory, not one meal went unsupplied during the year. Even when he was responsible for feeding two thousand orphans a day by faith, George testified later that no meal was ever more than thirty minutes late!

At the opening of the boys' house, George received his first legacy from a little boy who had saved some money during his fatal illness. Knowing that he would soon die, the boy asked that his savings, which amounted to a little more than $1.50, be sent to George Müller. He accepted it as his first legacy, and though but a small amount, he believed that God was placing His approval upon the new venture of the boys' house.

Many people asked George how he determined God's

will. He never undertook any venture, or the smallest expenditure, without feeling certain he was in God's will. In response George told them:

1. I seek at the beginning to get my heart into such a state that it has no will of its own in regard to a given matter. Nine-tenths of the difficulties are overcome when our hearts are ready to do the Lord's will, whatever it may be. When one is truly in this state, it is usually but a little way to the knowledge of what His will is.
2. Having done this, I do not leave the result to feeling or simple impressions. If so, I make myself liable to great delusions.
3. I seek the will of the Spirit of God through or in connection with the Word of God. The Spirit and the Word must be combined. If I look to the Spirit alone without the Word, I lay myself open to great delusions also.
4. Next I take into account providential circumstances. These plainly indicate God's will in connection with His Word and Spirit.
5. I ask God in prayer to reveal His will to me aright.
6. Thus through prayer to God, the study of the Word and reflection, I come to a deliberate judgment according to the best of my ability and knowledge, and if my mind is thus at peace, and continues so after two or three more petitions, I proceed accordingly. In trivial matters

and in transactions involving most important
issues, I have found this method always
effective.

Did this plan work? you might ask. Here is George's answer:
"I never remember," he wrote three years before his death,
"in all my Christian course, a period now [March 1895] of
sixty-nine years and four months, that I ever *sincerely and
patiently* sought to know the will of God by the teaching of
the Holy Ghost, through the instrumentality of the Word of
God, but I have been *always* directed rightly. But if honesty
of heart and uprightness before God were lacking, or if I did
not patiently wait upon God for instruction, or if I preferred
the counsel of my fellow men to the declarations of the Word
of the living God, I made great mistakes" (italics his).

When people asked why he undertook the work of the
Institution, George replied, "The first and primary object of
the Institution was, and still is, that God might be magnified
by the fact that the Orphans under my care were, and are,
provided with all they need only by prayer and faith, without anyone being asked by me or my fellow-laborers,
whereby it might be seen that God is *faithful still and hears
all prayers.*

eight

Each day for the next seven years, George needed to pray in daily supplies for the orphanages. Three houses had to be maintained, and about one hundred orphans required food and clothing. There was also considerable rent to pay, large daily expenditures, and the personal needs of the workers to be met. In addition, school maintenance, the work of the Institution, teachers' salaries, Sunday school operation, and missionary assistance all required a continual flow of money.

George never forgot how human he was—despite his numerous answers to prayer. And he recorded on January 15, 1838, that "my headache has become less severe since yesterday afternoon. But I am still far from being well. God is purifying me for His blessed service, and I will soon be restored to the work. Also He has restored a fervency of spirit which I have now enjoyed for the past three days. He has drawn my soul into real communion with Himself and into a holy desire to be more conformed to His dear Son."

He remarked, too, that when God gives a spirit of

prayer, it is easy to pray: "I spent about three hours in prayer over Psalms 64 and 65. In reference to that precious word, 'O thou that hearest prayer' (Psalm 65:2), I asked the Lord the following petitions and entreated Him to record them in heaven and to answer them:

1. That He would give me grace to glorify Him by a submissive and patient spirit under my affliction.
2. That the work of conversion through brother Craik and myself might not cease but go on as much now as when we first came to Bristol, and even more abundantly than then.
3. That He would give more spiritual prosperity to the church under our care than we have as yet enjoyed.
4. That His rich blessing would rest on this little work so that many may be converted through it and many benefitted by it.
5. That He would bring salvation to all the children under our care.
6. That He would supply the means to carry on these institutions and to enlarge them.

"I believe God has heard my prayers. He will make it manifest in His own good time that He has heard me. I have recorded my petitions that when God has answered them, His name will be glorified."

More than anything, George valued his daily prayer with the Lord. Despite his sickness early in 1838, he "entreated the Lord that this circumstance might not rob me of the precious communion I have had with Him the last three days—for this was the object at which Satan aimed. I also confessed my sin of irritability on account of the cold and sought to have my conscience cleansed through the blood of Jesus. He had mercy on me, and my peace was restored."

Even as he struggled with illness, George continued to look to God for the needs of the work. At times, the burden seemed almost too heavy to bear until one morning while kneeling in prayer, his eyes fell on a verse from Psalm 68: "A father of the fatherless." The verse leapt from the pages. "This word, 'A father of the fatherless,'" declared George, "contains enough encouragement to cast thousands of orphans, with all their needs, upon the loving heart of God." Henceforth, George refused to carry the burdens of the work, but to cast them on the Lord.

During June, however, God tested George's faith. Gifts suddenly stopped coming. Earlier, they had flowed forth like a mighty stream. George took the matter to the Lord. On July 17 and 18, special days of prayer were held from six to nine each evening to publicly commend the Boy's Orphan House to the Lord. George noted: "Our funds are now very low. About twenty pounds remain, and in a few days thirty pounds, at least, will be needed. But I purposely avoided saying anything about our present needs and only praised God and spoke about the abundance with which our gracious Father, 'the Father of the fatherless,' has supplied us. The hand of God will be clearly seen when He sends help."

A few days later, George wrote: "This evening I was walking in our little garden, meditating on Hebrews 13:8,

'Jesus Christ the same yesterday, and today, and forever.' All at once the present need of the Orphan-house was brought to my mind. Immediately I was led to say to myself, Jesus in His love and power has hitherto supplied me with what I have needed for the Orphans, and in the same unchangeable love and power He will provide with what I may need for the future. A flow of joy came into my soul."

The joy George felt announced a coming blessing: "About one minute later a letter was brought to me, enclosing a bill for twenty pounds." God's perfect timing proved a great encouragement to George.

The rest of 1838, George found his faith sorely tried. Many times there was not a single penny in the houses. Nevertheless, God continued to provide, strengthening George's faith in these smaller areas so that in the future he would be able to care for as many as two thousand children daily through the means of prayer.

Another crisis arose on September 18 when the funds were completely gone. George considered selling the items that could be done without in the homes. "This morning I had asked the Lord, if it might be, to prevent the necessity of our doing so." Again, the Lord responded quickly. That afternoon a lady from London, who was visiting in Bristol, brought a package with money in it from her daughter who had sent it several days earlier.

After the receipt of the money, George declared excitedly, "That the money had been so near for several days without being given, is a plain proof that it was in the heart of God to help us; but because He delights in the prayers of His children, He had allowed us to pray so long to try our faith and to make the answer so much the sweeter."

During this time George's health had declined, and friends urged him to go away for a rest. As usual, he refused, telling them: "I must remain to pass with my dear Orphans through the trial, though these dear ones know nothing about it, because their tables are as well supplied as when there was eight hundred pounds in the bank; and they have lack of nothing."

Over and over he would have to say, "The funds are exhausted." But the situation would change overnight. Funds might not have existed all day, but when nighttime came, there would be something on hand for the next day. George had faith—and trusted God for each day's needs.

During these trying times, George emphasized that "long before the trials came, I had more than once stated publicly that answers to prayer in the time of need—the manifestation of the hand of God stretched out for our help—were just the very ends for which the Institution was established."

Sometimes with many resources, but more often in poverty, George's faith carried the orphanages. Frequently in times of great distress, the money would arrive at the very moment of prayer or as he was reading the list of needs for the day. George's trust in "the Father of the fatherless" was so certain that he never turned a child away. On August 8, 1839, he announced, "Though there is no money in hand, yet are we so little discouraged that we have received today one orphan boy, and have given notice for the admission of six other children, which will bring the number up to 98 altogether."

The ways God chose to answer George's prayers are instructive. Frequently gifts came in at the very instant of prayer. George noted on March 5, 1839, "Whilst I was in prayer, Q. sent a check for seven pounds." And at the close of 1839, he sums up the bounteous blessing of God, reporting, "For the Orphan Houses, without any one having been asked by us, over 3,067 pounds has been given entirely as the result of prayer to God, from the commencement of the work to December 9, 1839."

Even as the next year commenced, there was not enough money to supply the orphanages for one day. A telling incident occurred that day which displayed George's character. After the usual Watch Night service, close to 1:00 A.M. on New Year's Day, a friend handed George a sealed envelope with money in it. George knew him to be in debt and refused to accept the gift. He says of the incident: "I resolved, therefore, without opening the paper to return it. This was done when I knew there was not enough in hand to meet the expenses of the day."

Within seven hours, a brother brought five pounds for the orphans. "Observe, the brother is led to bring it at once," George reported. The Lord honored George's faith in returning the money he knew was needed to pay his brother's debts more than the orphans needed it.

George continually learned new things about the Lord, and he repeatedly experienced new aspects of prayer, and so was qualified to speak to others, not concerning speculation, theory, or doctrinal belief, but of long, varied, and successful personal experience. Sometimes he met those to whom his courageous, childlike trust in God was a mystery; and occasionally someone with unbelief would question him: "What would he do if God did not send help? What if a meal-time actually came with no food, and no money to procure it; or if clothing were worn out, and nothing to replace it?"

To all these questions George always had one answer ready: that such a failure on God's part is inconceivable, and must therefore be put among the impossibilities. He realized, however, that people must meet certain conditions for God to answer their prayers. First of all, the seeking person must come to God in the right spirit and attitude.

Five overall conditions for prayer were always uppermost in George's mind:

1. Entire dependence upon the merits and mediation of the Lord Jesus Christ as the only ground of any claim for blessing.
2. Separation from all known sin. If we regard iniquity in our hearts the Lord will not hear us, for it would be sanctioning sin.
3. Faith in God's word of promise as confirmed by His oath. Not to believe Him is to make Him both a liar and a perjurer.
4. Asking in accordance with His will. Our motives must be godly: we must not seek any gift of God to consume it upon our own lusts.
5. Importunity in supplication. There must be waiting on God and waiting for God, as the husbandman has long patience to wait for the harvest.

Where these conditions did not exist, George realized that God could not answer prayer because He would dishonor Himself and cause damage to the person praying. If God encouraged those who came to Him in their own name, or in a self-righteous, self-seeking, and disobedient spirit, He would be setting a premium upon continuance in sin. These conditions for prevailing prayer exist, George believed, because they are necessary both to God's character and our good.

George saw the vital relation of prayer to holiness and endeavored to teach this truth to those around him. He would say, too, that all prayer prevails only in the measure of our real, even if not conscious, unity with the Lord Jesus Christ as the ground of our approach, and in the degree of our dependence on Him as the medium of our access to God.

Perhaps the most important key to prevailing prayer, he would stress, is that prayer must be offered in faith and that the answer to such prayer can be recognized and received only on the plane of faith. We must maintain the believing attitude, expecting the blessing, and being ready to receive it in God's way and time and form, not our own.

Since he expected God to answer his prayers, George was not really surprised when the answers came. At a particularly crucial time in November 1840, a woman gave ten pounds for the orphans, and George rejoiced in this gift, but he also knew beforehand that God would provide it. Help had been so long delayed that in one of the houses there was no bread, and none of the children had any milk, nor was there money to buy it. When the gift arrived, it was only a few minutes before the milkman's cart was due!

Earlier, George had recorded this attitude about prayer: "The Lord, to show His continued care over us, raises up new helpers. They that trust in the Lord shall never be confounded.

Some who helped for a while may fall asleep in Jesus; others grow cold in the service of the Lord; others be as desirous as ever to help, but no longer able. But in leaning upon God, the Living God alone, we are beyond disappointment and beyond being forsaken because of death, or want of means, or want of love, or because of the claims of other work. How precious to have learned, in any measure, to be content to stand with God alone in the world, and to know that surely no good thing shall be withheld from us, while we walk uprightly!"

One singular offering in response to prayer came in March 1839. George had given a copy of the annual report to one of his brothers in the work. This brother had been greatly moved to pray by reading it. He knew that his sister (also one of the group) owned some expensive jewelry, including a heavy gold chain, a pair of gold bracelets, and a superb ring set with fine stones, and he tried to persuade her to do something useful with her jewelry. He pointed out the worthlessness of these ornaments to the world and urged her to give them for the orphan work, which she did.

The jewelry was given at a particularly trying time, and George's heart rejoiced when the pieces came. The proceeds of the sale were used to help meet the expenses of a whole week, and also to help pay the salaries due the workers. Before he sold the diamond ring, George wrote with it upon the window pane of his own room one of the Lord's titles: Jehovah Jireh. After that, whenever he went through a critical time without money or goods, George would glance at the window pane and remember that this name for God carried the promise that the Lord will provide.

As was his custom, George summed up his prayer experiences of 1840:

1. Notwithstanding multiplied trials of faith, the orphans have lacked nothing.
2. Instead of being disappointed in my expectations or work, the reverse has been true, such trials being seen to be needful to demonstrate that the Lord is my Helper (and the orphans') in our times of need.
3. Such a way of living brings the Lord very near, as one who daily inspects the need that He may send the more timely aid.
4. Such constant, instant reliance upon divine help does not so absorb the mind in temporal things as to unfit for spiritual employments and enjoyments; but rather prompts to habitual communion with the Lord and His Word.
5. Other children of God may not be called to a similar work, but are called to a like faith, and may experience similar interposition if they live according to His will and seek His help.
6. The incurring of debt, being unscriptural, is a sin needing confession and abandonment if we desire unhindered fellowship with God.

In the same year, the people in charge of the Scripture Knowledge Institution added new responsibilities: that of distributing Christian books and tracts. As usual, with additional needs, the group continued to pray and seek God for the literature, and God supplied even more than before. The supply always kept up with the need.

Many times the "responders" and "givers" to the prayer requests also felt a timeliness when they prayed. Frequently, without any hint being given them from other people that there was a special need, their hearts would be impressed in prayer to God that there was an emergency requiring prompt assistance.

An example of such a happening occurred in June 1841. George received fifty pounds that day with a note: "I am not concerned at my having been prevented for so many days from sending this money; I am confident it has not been needed."

George was also impressed with the gift's timeliness: "This last sentence is remarkable. It is now nearly three years since our funds were for the first time exhausted, and only at this period, since then, could it have been said in truth, so far as I remember, that a donation of fifty pounds was not needed.

"From the beginning of July 1838, till now," George continued, " there never had been a period when we so abounded as when this donation came; for there were then, in the orphan fund and the other funds, between two and three hundred pounds! The words of our brother are so much the more remarkable as, on four former occasions, when he likewise gave considerable donations, we were always in need, yea, great need, which he afterwards knew from the printed accounts." George knew that when he prayed, the Lord would send the answers through another praying person.

On January 12, 1841, after he had had to delay printing

his yearly report because of a lack of funds, George noted that the Lord supplied this need plus an additional five thousand dollars for missionary work. Concerning this gift, the largest they had yet received, he wrote: "In all my experience I have found that if I could only settle a certain thing to be done was according to the will of God, that means were soon obtained to carry it into effect." The Lord never failed him, even though at times he endured great poverty. Always God brought an abundant supply in answer to prevailing prayer.

nine

One day in 1841 when George had taken only a shilling from the house box, a lady came with two-pence, telling him, "It is but a trifle, but I must give it." It so happened that one of the pennies was needed to make up the amount of money necessary to buy bread.

A single penny was needed a week later to fill out the dinner menu, but none was available. When the girls' box was opened, one penny rolled out! "Even the gift of a penny," declared George, "was thus evidently under the ordering of our kind Father."

At the end of the year, he affirmed, "We are now brought to the close of the sixth year of this work, having in hand only the money which has been put by for the rent; but during the whole of this year we have been supplied with all that was needed."

During the next three years, George literally fed the orphans out of God's hand. The supply was almost like that of manna for the Israelites in the wilderness because it had to be gathered each day. There was scarcely anything left over from one day to another. Often money had to be prayed in before breakfast could be eaten or the evening meal finished.

George's faith was so strong that however much the need, he rested calmly in divine assurance that God's hand would contain an abundant supply at the proper time. He refused to worry—and had long since made up his mind not to give in to worry. Though he might be deeply concerned, he never fretted at delay in receiving answers to his requests.

George showed his typical attitude on February 15, 1842: " I sat peacefully down to give myself to meditation over the Word, considering that was now my service, though I knew not whether there was a morsel of bread for tea in any of the houses, but being assured that the Lord would provide. For through grace my mind is so fully assured of the faithfulness of the Lord, that in the midst of the greatest need, I am enabled in peace to go about my other work. Indeed, did not the Lord give me this, which is the result of trusting in Him, I should be scarcely able to work at all." He had fixed his mind on God and would not be moved; at the right time, the money or food would arrive.

March 19 began in great need—even poverty. Only seven shillings had come in during three days. George noted urgently: "There was not one ray of light as far as natural prospects." Thus he proposed to his workers that the day be set aside for prayer. When they met at 10:30, immediately three separate people brought in twenty-one shillings. In the evening a similar session of prayer was called since three shillings were still needed. Before the evening service was over the three shillings arrived, plus an additional three.

Week by week God led George into deeper lessons of trust, always closing the day's trust sessions with a speedy answer. An illustration of the Lord's "speedy answers" came on a March morning. George reported that "this morning our poverty, which now has lasted for several months, became exceedingly great. I left my house a few minutes after seven to go to the Orphan Houses to see whether there was enough money to buy milk. I prayed that the Lord would have mercy on us, even as a father has mercy on his children. I reminded Him of the consequences that would result, both in the lives of believers and unbelievers, if we had to give up the work because of lack of money, and that He therefore would not permit it to fail." As he walked and prayed, he "met a brother on his way to work. I greeted him and walked on, but he ran after me and gave me one pound for the orphans. Thus the Lord speedily answered my prayer."

Week by week God led George into deeper lessons of trust, always closing the day's trust sessions with a speedy answer. But on April 12, George confessed, "We were never in greater need than today, when I received one hundred pounds from the East Indies. It is impossible to describe the joy in God it gave me. My prayer this morning had been that our Father would now at last send larger sums of money. I was not in the least surprised or excited when this donation came, for I took it as the answer to prayer and had been long looked for."

People often asked George during these faith-trying times how he managed to build such a strong faith in God. He told them that he tried to keep his faith in God strong not only for daily supplies of food for the orphans and money for the missionary work, but also for the spiritual concerns of the world.

He also stressed to them: "Let not Satan deceive you in making you think you could not have the same faith, but that it is only for persons situated as I am. When I lose such a thing as a key, I ask the Lord to direct me to it, and I look for an answer to my prayer; when a person with whom I have an appointment does not come, I ask the Lord to be pleased to hasten him to me, and I look for an answer. Thus in all my temporal and spiritual concerns, I pray to the Lord and expect an answer to my requests; and may not you do the same?"

In giving advice gained through the daily trials of his faith, George offered certain rules profitable for Christians to follow and be strengthened in their faith. Simply put, they are:

1. Carefully read the Bible and meditate on it. Through reading the Word of God, and especially through meditation on it, we become acquainted with the nature and character of God. Besides God's holiness and justice, we realize what a kind, loving, gracious, merciful, mighty, wise, and faithful Father He is. Therefore, in poverty, affliction, death of loved ones, difficulty in service, or financial need, we will rest on the ability of God to help us. We have learned from the Word that God is almighty in power, infinite in wisdom, and ready to help and deliver His people. Reading the Word of

God, together with meditation on it, is an excellent way to strengthen faith.

2. We must maintain an upright heart and a good conscience and not knowingly and habitually indulge in things which are contrary to the mind of God. How can I possibly continue to act in faith if I grieve the Lord and detract from His glory and honor? All my confidence in God and all my leaning on Him in the hour of trial will be gone if I have a guilty conscience and yet continue in sin. If I cannot trust in God because of a guilty conscience, my faith is weakened. With every fresh trial, faith either increases by trusting God and getting help, or it decreases by not trusting Him. A habit of self-dependence is either defeated or encouraged. If we trust in God, we do not trust in ourselves, our fellowmen, circumstances, or in anything else. If we do trust in one or more of these, we do not trust in God.

3. If we desire our faith to be strengthened, we should not shrink from opportunities where our faith may be tried. The more I am in a position to be tried in faith, the more I will have the opportunity of seeing God's help and deliverance. Every fresh instance in which He helps and delivers me will increase my faith. We should not shrink from situations, positions, or circumstances in which our faith may be tried, but he should cheerfully embrace them

as opportunities to see the hand of God stretched out in help and deliverance. Thus our faith will be strengthened.

4. The last important point for the strengthening of our faith is that we let God work for us and do not work a deliverance of our own. When a trial of faith comes, we are naturally inclined to distrust God and to trust in ourselves, in our friends, or in circumstances. We would rather work a deliverance of our own than simply look to God and wait for His help. But if we do not patiently wait for God's help or if we work a deliverance of our own, then at the next trial of our faith we will have the same problem. We will again be inclined to try and deliver ourselves. With every fresh trial, our faith will decrease. On the contrary, if we stand firm in order to see the salvation of God, trusting in Him alone, our faith will be increased.

Finally, the believer "must give God time to work, if he would have his faith strengthened," George emphasized. Each time we see God's Hand stretched out on our behalf in the hour of trial, our faith will be increased even more. The Lord will show His willingness to help and deliver us at the perfect time.

George believed that scriptural principles may be used to overcome the difficulties in business or in any calling. Since they are "strangers and pilgrims" in the earth, God's children can expect to have difficulty in the world. But God has provided a way for them to triumph over circumstances through the promises in His Word. George stressed that "all difficulties may be overcome by acting according to the Word of God."

Some of his personal trials happened when his brother and father died. George poignantly shared that "I had no evidence that they were saved. But I dare not say that they are lost, for I do not know. My soul was perfectly at peace under this trial, which is one of the greatest a believer can experience. I laid hold of that promise, 'Shall not the Judge of all the earth do right?' (Genesis 18:25). This word, together with the whole character of God, as He has revealed Himself in His holy Word, settled all questionings. I believed what He has said concerning Himself and have been at peace ever since concerning this matter."

By December 1, 1842, the orphanage workers and George basked in an unusual prosperity. Money and supplies had flowed in uninterrupted for several months as they were needed. But there was never too much nor too little—always just the right amount would come. Yet on this day, there was only five shillings for needlework and the exact amount for the necessary milk. They could not purchase their usual quantity of bread.

George realized what people said about his walk of faith: "Someone may ask, 'Why don't you buy the bread on credit? What does it matter whether you pay immediately for it or at the end of the month? Since the Orphan Houses are the work of the Lord, can't you trust Him to supply you with money to pay the bills from the butcher, baker, and grocer?' My reply is: "If this work is the work of God, then He is surely able and willing to provide for it. He will not necessarily provide at the time we think that there is a need. But when there is real need, He will not fail us. We may and should trust in the Lord to supply us with what we require at present, so that there may be no reason to go into debt."

He knew that he could purchase whatever the work required on credit, but each time a new need arose, he would need to use more credit. This method, according to George, would negate constant dependence on the Lord. He understood that faith is maintained and strengthened only by exercise. If he didn't face challenges and difficulties, his faith would get weaker and weaker.

George also sought to practice the scriptural principle, "Owe no man any thing," found in Romans 13:8. By going into debt, he would say, a believer does not adhere to the Word of God.

He expressed concern that his ministry continue to be a testimony to God's goodness. George wished "to show the world and the Church that God is ready to help, comfort, and answer the prayers of those who trust in Him. We need not go to our fellowmen or to the ways of the world. God is both able and willing to supply us with all we need in His service."

He added, "Through the printed accounts of this ministry, many have been converted. We consider it our precious privilege to continue to wait upon the Lord only instead of buying goods on credit or borrowing money from kind friends. As God gives us grace we will look to Him only, although from meal to meal we have to depend on Him. God is now in the tenth year of feeding these orphans, and He has never allowed them to go hungry. He will care for them in the future also."

Deeply aware of his own helplessness and dependence on the Lord, George rejoiced in the trials of faith God had allowed in his life. Sanctioning everything he had gone through, he emphasized that "through the grace of God my soul is in peace, although day after day we have to wait on the Lord for our daily bread."

The year 1843, even as the one before, was one of trials and triumphs of faith. In June there was no money, but before the close of each day, prayer brought in needed food, money, and supplies. Even his own personal needs were supplied by the Lord on this "one day only" basis.

For several months, George asked God daily to send a gift a lady had promised in 1842. He received the answer on March 8, 1843. As he explained: "Day after day now has passed away and the money did not come. . .whilst day by day I brought my petition before the Lord that He would bless this sister. At last, on the one hundred and thirty-fourth day since I daily besought the Lord about this matter, I received a letter from the sister, informing me that the five hundred pounds had been paid into the hands of my bankers."

The month before, George wrote: "We had one pound fourteen shillings available to meet the expenses of this day. But since this was not enough, I asked the Lord for help; and this morning's mail brought me two pounds from Stafford. We now have enough for this day."

George added: "God's timing is always perfect. Why did this money not come a few days sooner or later? Because the Lord wanted to help us by it, and He influenced the donor just then, not sooner or later, to send it. Surely, all who know the Lord must see His hand in this work. I do not mean to say that it would be acting against the precepts of the Lord to seek for help in His work by personal and individual requests to believers. But I operate the ministry this way for the benefit of the Church at large. I cheerfully bear the trials and the precious joys of this life of faith if at least some of my fellow believers might see that a child of God does have power with Him by prayer and faith. That the Lord should use for so glorious a service one as unfaithful and unworthy as I am, can only be ascribed to the riches of His grace. He uses the most unlikely instruments so that the honor may be His alone."

God now pointed George in a new direction. Beginning on March 31, 1843, when George called at the orphan houses to make arrangements for the day, a worker told him that a Miss G., who lived in 4 Wilson Street, had planned to give their house to George for another orphan house.

A flood of emotions surged through George. Was it possible that God wanted him to take on yet another orphan house? "When I came home this matter greatly occupied my mind," George wrote. "I could not but ask the Lord again and again whether He would have me to open another Orphan house, and whether the time was now come that I should serve Him still more extensively on the matter."

As George carefully considered this turn of events, he realized they had received more admission applications than they had room for. Fifteen of the infant house children were old enough to be promoted to the girls' house. Until now, no other houses on Wilson Street had been available for rent. Almost at the same time, two sisters offered to take care of the new house if and when it opened—and in the bank, George had three hundred pounds of the recently received gift which could be used to furnish the new house.

Although the circumstances pointed in the direction of a new house, George had to be certain of God's will. He explained: "I therefore gave myself to prayer. I prayed day after day, without saying anything to any human being. I prayed two and twenty days without mentioning it to my dear wife. On that day on which I had come to the conclusion to establish another Orphan House, I received fifty pounds from A.B. What a striking confirmation that the Lord would help though the necessities should increase more and more."

George understood what this new burden would mean. For five years he had trusted each day for supplies, and the new house would only increase the needs. Even as he considered the ramifications of this new responsibility, he knew God was leading him forward, requiring an increased faith and trust in Him. George never tired of "this precious way of depending upon the Lord from day to day."

As George prayed about the new house, a German woman asked him to return for a visit to Germany. She had recently been blessed by his work and felt his influence would greatly benefit his native country of Germany. It seemed unwise for him to leave at that time since it would require many hundreds of pounds to be left for the orphans' overseers as well as money for the trip. Further, he wanted to publish a German edition of his life story, *A Narrative of Some of the Lord's Dealings with Mr. George Müller.*

It would cost between a hundred and two hundred pounds simply to publish the book. Yet he realized that, however great the obstacles, if the Lord wanted him to go, he would go. So, he wrote, "I could not but pray about it. I could not but feel drawn to go to Germany in love of the Lord and in pity towards the poor Church of Christ in that country." George thought about the few truly converted ministers he had found there and in Prussia as a young man. His faith began to urge him forward.

With great joy, he wrote: "I had a secret satisfaction in the greatness of the difficulties. So far from being cast down on account of them, they delighted my soul. I did nothing but pray. Prayer and faith helped me over the difficulties." From a human standpoint, receiving the necessary funds appeared bleak. But as George left the matter with the Lord, he felt overwhelmed with calm: "My soul is at peace. The Lord's time is not yet come; but when it is come, He will blow away all these obstacles."

Less than fifteen minutes after George had prayed on July 12, God sent in 702 pounds, 3 shillings, and 7 pence. And in early August, after waiting on the Lord for 50 days, George and his wife left for Germany.

In Stuttgart, George attempted to reform the strict Baptist Church in the city but met with severe opposition. Although the visit seemed a failure, some wonderful blessings were also connected with it. While he was in Stuttgart, the way opened for him to translate his book into German. Four thousand copies were printed before he sailed for Bristol the next February.

As he returned to Bristol in 1844, George began praying again for funds to open the fourth orphan house. Before leaving for Germany, he had felt certain that God was opening the way for the house to be operated. For nearly ten years, he had rented houses for his orphans, and "had never had any desire to build an Orphan House. On the contrary, I decidedly preferred spending the means which might come in for present necessities, and desired rather to enlarge the work according to the means the Lord might be pleased to give. Thus it was till the end of October 1845 when I was led to consider this matter in a light in which I had never done before."

The Lord, however, was preparing to thrust George into a faith venture which would surpass even his greatest dreams. God had carefully schooled him with lessons in trust, and now that George had learned how to believe for daily supplies, and for months had literally been fed meal by meal from God's hand, the "Father of the fatherless" was going to open a new and untried door for him.

ten

G eorge was willing to pass through any door the Lord set ajar for him. On October 31, 1845, the matter of a new orphan house came to a head. When he was about to rent the vacated house near his other properties, a man wrote stating that the orphan houses were a detriment to the neighboring house owners. The letter's remarks were courteous and kind, but nevertheless firm. The man said that in various ways the neighbors were inconvenienced by the Orphan Houses on Wilson Street, and he trusted George to make a wise decision concerning the situation.

George had not counted on this new development in his plans. But he did wish to live peacefully with his neighbors, so he took the matter to the Lord in prayer. He carefully weighed the pros and cons concerning a move from Wilson Street. To move, he knew, meant to build, and up until this time he had not thought it God's will to take this step of faith. But God's time was about to arrive, and he had learned to step when God's hour struck, however great the problem or vexing the difficulty.

Evaluating this new development, George said, "I was very busy that week, and I had scarcely any time to consider it further. On Monday morning, however, I set apart some hours for prayerful consideration of the subject. I wrote down the reasons which appeared desirable that the Orphan Houses should be moved from Wilson Street, and the reasons against moving."

Some of the reasons why the Houses should be moved were:

1. The inconvenience caused the neighbors by the children's noise during playtime: "This complaint is neither without foundation nor unjust, although one could not find fault with the dear children on account of it. It would probably give me a headache if I lived next door to the Orphan Houses. I therefore should do to others as I want them to do for me."

2. The large numbers of residents in the houses has prevented the drains from working properly, and it has often affected the water in one or two of the neighbors' houses. "These words, 'Let not then your good be evil spoken of' (Romans 14:16), and 'Let your moderation [willingness to yield] be known unto all men' (Philippians 4:5), seemed two important portions of the Word of God to be acted upon in this matter."

3. "We have no proper playgrounds on Wilson Street. Our playground is only large enough for

the children of one house at a time." They
were forced to stagger the use of the playground.

4. "No ground is available for a garden near the
   Orphan Houses. By moving from Wilson Street
   and obtaining premises surrounded by farmland,
   we would be able to benefit the children. They
   would have a better opportunity for practical
   labor, and it would give the boys an occupation
   more suitable for them than knitting."

5. "The country air would be much better for the
   health of the orphans than the polluted air of the
   city."

6. "In times of sickness we are too confined in the
   houses on Wilson Street. We do not have a
   single spare room in any of the houses.
   Although the Lord has mercifully helped us
   through such times in the past, yet it has not
   been without inconvenience. We sometimes
   have more children in one room than is desirable for good health. Even when there is no
   sickness, it would be desirable to have more
   room."

Confronted with the various reasons as to why they should
move, George stated "The more I have considered the matter, the more I am persuaded that no ordinary large house,
built only to accommodate ten people at most, will be suitable for a charitable institution of any considerable size.
There seemed to me, therefore, no other choice but to build."

George saw three main problems in building (as opposed to staying):

1. The large amount of money required, "which could be spent for the orphans' present needs."
2. "The pilgrim character of the Christian seems to be lost in building a permanent structure."
3. "It will take a great deal of time to make the necessary arrangements for it."

However, George realized that these objections would hold true only if he proceeded to build needlessly. But he knew that was not the case; the need to build was considerable. So one by one, he responded to the objections until he saw clearly that it was the Lord's will for them to build their own structure for the work.

God's time had come for George to step out on the divine promises and build. He had carefully weighed the reasons for and against building. As he explained: "After I had spent a few hours in prayer and consideration over the subject, I began to see that the Lord was leading me to build. His intentions were to benefit the orphans and better order of the whole work. Furthermore, He wanted to show that He could and would provide large sums for those who need them and trust in Him for them."

George added: "During no period had the number of applications for the admission of orphans been greater than just before I was led to think about building."

The next day George and his wife agreed to pray together each morning about the building. "We continued meeting for prayer morning by morning for fifteen days," he related, "but not a single donation came; yet my heart was not discouraged. The more I prayed, the more I was assured that the Lord would give the means."

A special gift arrived on December 13 when a Christian architect offered to draw the plans and superintend the building without payment. George took this offer as further proof that God was directing his prayers and intentions toward building.

The funds began to come in slowly, though George had not publicly announced his plans to build. George knew that it required faith to care for the 130 children then in the homes, and that it would take greater faith to feed and clothe 300.

He confided, "Sufficiently large premises to accommodate three hundred children would be needed, together with a large piece of ground near Bristol for the building and a small farm. This would cost at least ten thousand pounds. I was not discouraged by this but trusted in God." George and his co-workers continued to meet in prayer every morning for fifteen days, but not a single donation came in.

"My heart was not discouraged. The more I prayed, the more assured I was that the Lord would provide. It is as if I had already seen the new premises actually before me. Since the beginning of the Scriptural Knowledge Institution, God has led me forward and enlarged the work without my seeking after it. My only motives are the honor and glory of God, the welfare of the Church, the physical and spiritual welfare of destitute orphans, and the welfare of all those who would take care of them."

Moreover, he added, "After praying again and again

about the matter, I still remained in perfect peace. I therefore decided it was assuredly God's will that I should go forward." George continued to pray and wait on God for finances. Even though no money had come in, his certainty increased that God, in His own time and in His own way, would provide for the work.

Certain verses in particular seemed to speak to George at this time: "My brethren, count it all joy when ye fall into divers temptations; Knowing this, that the trying of your faith worketh patience. But let patience have her perfect work, that ye may be perfect and entire, wanting nothing" (James 1:2-4). He noted that "these words spoke to my heart about building the Orphan House. I asked the Lord to increase my faith and sustain my patience. I knew that I needed patience as well as faith."

After praying for thirty-six days, George received one thousand pounds for building the house. "It was the largest single donation I had ever received," he remarks, "but I was as calm and quiet as if I had only received one shilling because I was expecting to receive an answer to my prayers. Even if five thousand pounds or ten thousand pounds had been given to me, it would not have surprised me."

On January 31, 1846, George went to see a piece of land that seemed available for the building. This was the eighty-ninth day since he had begun to call upon God for a building, and he thought God would soon furnish adequate property. He desired about seven acres close to Bristol. God had the land for him, and in due time—after more testing of his faith —the land would be provided.

"On February 3," George reported, "I saw the land on

Ashley Down. It is the best of all I have seen." The following day he began negotiations for the property. He went to visit the owner, but he was not home. When he made an appointment with him the next day, the owner told George that he had been awakened about three o'clock and could not sleep for two hours.

George continued: "While he was thus lying awake, his mind was all the time occupied about the piece of land, and he determined that if I should apply for it, he would not only let me have it, but for 120 pounds an acre instead of 200, the price he had previously asked for it. How good is the Lord!" Thus he was able to purchase the land for $2800 less than he would have the night before.

After the land was bought, George continued his daily time of praying specifically about the building funds. Step by step he waited for the Lord to supply all that was needed in the construction of such a large building.

Gifts varying in size from a farthing to five and six hundred pounds made George's heart glad. On January 25, 1847, he wrote: "Therefore with increased earnestness I have given myself unto prayer, importuning the Lord that He would speedily send the remainder of the amount, and I have increasingly of late felt that the time is drawing near." Fourteen months and three weeks had now passed since George Müller first began asking God for a new building.

That same morning, he reported, "About an hour after I had prayed, the sum of two thousand pounds was given to me for the building fund. I cannot describe the joy I had in God when I received this donation. I have waited 447 days upon God for the amount we needed. How great is the blessing the soul obtains by trusting in God and by waiting patiently. From December 10, 1845 to January 25, 1847, I have received, solely in answer to prayer, 9,285 pounds. The Lord is willing to give what will be needed once the new Orphan House is built, although the expenses will be about 2,500 pounds a year more than they were before."

George's joy that morning was so great, he wrote, "All I could do was sit before God and admire Him, like David in 2 Samuel 7. Finally, I threw myself flat on my face and burst forth in thanksgivings to God and surrendered my heart afresh to Him for His blessed service."

Other gifts soon followed, among them two thousand pounds, then another one thousand pounds. And on July 5, 1847, when 11,062 pounds had been donated, work on the building finally began.

Realizing that he had sought the Lord daily for 607 days for the building fund, George rejoiced in the Lord's timing and provision. The last gift received at that time came from a man who brought the money in notes so that his bankers would not discover his generosity.

Amazingly, after completion of the building, all the expenses paid, and the trustees organized, a balance of 776 pounds remained. George saw the provision "a manifest proof that the Lord can not only supply us with all we need in His service simply in answer to prayer, but that He can also give us even more than we need."

All of these gifts were received from the hand of God through George's prayers. He prayed definitely and diligently. God answered just as specifically. In addition to praying in the building funds, George also bore the burden of caring for the houses on Wilson Street and their 130 children. Never once did he despair of the Lord's willingness and ability to give. He knew he was in the center of God's will, and asking and receiving were natural complements.

June 18, 1849, proved to be a memorable day. The orphans were transferred from the rented houses on Wilson Street to the new house on Ashley Down. The building had been in progress for two years. Throughout the year other children arrived until by May 26 of the following year, there were 275 children in the house. This number brought the total number of children connected with the institution to 308. Each of these daily depended upon George's prayers for their sustenance.

Noting on July 21 certain requests, George asked God for four specific things: for his own personal needs, for the building fund, for the orphanage on Wilson Street, and for the Institution. That same day, a man from Devonshire came to visit the orphanage and donated twenty pounds; he specified that it was for the four identical things about which George had been talking to God. Exulting in the Lord's accurate provision, George wrote, "Thus I received, at the very moment that I had been asking God, four answers to my prayers."

By Saturday, June 23, after the move to Ashley Down, God began supplying the needs in a marvelous way. A man accompanying George on a tour through the new home exclaimed, "These children must consume a great deal of provisions." While he spoke, he drew from his wallet one hundred notes. On the same day, six casks of treacle (molasses) and six loaves of sugar arrived. Then the overseers learned that someone had just purchased a thousand pounds of rice for the children.

"So bountifully has the Lord been pleased to help of late, that I have not only been able to meet all the extraordinary heavy expenses connected with moving—filling the storehouses—but I have more than five hundred pounds in hand to begin house-keeping in the new Orphan House," George wrote. In addition, he noted, "After all the many and long-continued seasons of great trial of faith for thirteen years and two months, during which the orphans were in Wilson Street, the Lord dismisses us from thence in comparative abundance. His name be praised."

In fact, the Lord's supply had been so ample that the new house was nearly filled to capacity with orphans and with provisions. Now George's faith expanded to search out new horizons. If he could care for three hundred orphans through faith and prayer, why could he not care for a thousand children?

George was merely on the threshold of what God had in store for him.

eleven

On December 5, 1850, George celebrated an anniversary of sorts. He wrote, "It is now sixteen years and nine months this evening since I began the Scriptural Knowledge Institution for Home and Abroad. It is so large that I have not only disbursed since its commencement about fifty thousand pounds sterling, but that also the current expenses amount to above six thousand pounds a year. I did 'open my mouth wide' this evening fifteen years ago, and the Lord has filled it. The new Orphan House is filled by three hundred orphans. My labor is abundant."

George felt his heart literally consumed with passion for God and for orphans. At Christmas time in 1850, he declared, "I have served Satan much in my younger years, and I desire now with all my might to serve God during the remaining days of my earthly pilgrimage. I am forty-five years and three months old. Every day decreases the number of days that I have to stay on earth. I therefore desire with all my might to work. There are vast multitudes of orphans to be provided for."

Soon the idea of another house, even larger, began to burn in his soul. He wrote, "By the help of God I shall continue day by day to wait upon Him in prayer concerning this thing till He shall bid me act."

On January 14, 1851, George reviewed his earlier list of the pros and cons of building a new house to care for seven hundred more children, and as before, faith prevailed, and he declared that God would enable him to carry it through.

A couple weeks later, he sensed that God would be honored by his letting others know of the idea. He set the sum of thirty-five thousand pounds as the amount to be received before beginning to build. In May of that year he let people know of his plans. Realizing that the financial need was large, his heart leaped with secret joy, "for the greater the difficulty to be overcome, the more it would be seen to the glory of God how much can be done by prayer and faith."

Immediately gifts began to come in, the first being only sixpence, donated by one of the orphans. While reading Hebrews 6:15, "And so after he had patiently endured, he obtained the promise," George's heart gained strength. He had become somewhat discouraged with the slowness and the smallness of the gifts as they arrived.

His faith had to stand many trials in 1851. But in March of that year, he received encouragement by a gift of 999 pounds, and when the accounts for the twelve months were closed, the fund stood at 3,530 pounds, which included the 776 pounds left from the first building fund.

At this time 360 orphans were waiting to be admitted, and as the applications arrived, George's faith increased correspondingly. For where there was a need, he knew God would surely supply. At the beginning of 1853, several Christians banded together, promising approximately $40,500 to be distributed among the various funds, $30,000 of which was to go into the building fund.

With this promised provision, George realized there was no limit to God's willingness and ability to provide large donations. And as the money increased, George began looking for suitable property, but when none was found close by the first house, he decided to construct two buildings instead of one. The first one would house 400 girls, and the other, 300 boys. He had the funds on hand to construct the first building, so he decided to go ahead with the first house. By that time, some 715 orphans sought admission to the home.

Donations began to pour in from nearly every corner of the world. George's book had been translated into several languages, and the story of his work had spread from country to country.

In spite of the numerous large gifts that flowed in continuously, George remained a faithful servant in the smaller things. He wrote on October 12, 1852, "By the sale of rags and bones, twelve shillings, sixpence. I copy literally from the receipt book. We seek to make the best of everything. As a steward of public money, I feel it right that even these articles should be turned into money; nor could we expect answers to our prayers if knowingly there were any waste allowed in connection with the work."

During these times of a larger vision and work, God led George to trust Him day by day for supplies. Speaking of two weeks during the Christmas holidays of 1852, George said, 'We had nothing in advance of our wants. Means came in only as they were required for pressing needs. We ask no human being for help. We depend alone upon God."

While the work of building the new house was in progress, George kept his requests before the Lord daily. Large gifts came in, one for fifteen thousand dollars and another for twenty thousand dollars. He also received an offer to fill the three hundred large windows in the house with glass.

Concerning this gift, George observed: "It is worthy of note that the glass was not contracted for this time, as in the case of the House already built. This, no doubt, was under the ordering of our Heavenly Father."

About one year before the building was finished, approximately $150,000 was on hand for the expense. On one occasion, while he was examining the 150 gas burners, George felt constrained to return home at once. Reaching his home, he found a check for 1,000 pounds from a person who "concluded it would be good and profitable to invest a little in the Orphan Houses."

Finally, on November 12, 1857, seven years after the idea had first burned in George's soul, the New Orphan House, No. 2, was opened. He wrote on that day: "The long looked-for and long prayed-for day has now arrived when the desire of my heart was granted to me, to be able to open the house for four hundred additional orphans. How precious this was to me having day by day prayed for a blessing for seven years."

When the house was opened, a balance remained of approximately twenty-three hundred pounds. This sum was to form the basis for contributions to build the third house. George envisioned a structure that would house three hundred children.

Planning to build the third house by the first house, George could not find the right property nearby. After much searching, he located some higher-priced land across the road from the existing facilities. The price was high, more than sixteen thousand dollars, but since it was so close to the other buildings, he thought it wise to invest God's money in it.

Then, since many applications had come in, it was decided to make this building large enough to care for 450 children instead of the original 300. In confirmation of this decision, a gift arrived shortly of 7,000 pounds, to be followed by another of 1,700 pounds. Glass was again promised for the 309 windows, and in July 1859, the builders began their work.

God began to pour funds out lavishly to care for the children while the house was being constructed. Indeed, the expense credit fund held more than $45,000 before the third house was occupied.

On March 12, 1862, the house opened. George was full of joy on this occasion. He recorded: "It was in November 1850 that my mind became exercised about enlarging the orphan work from 300 to 1,000 orphans, and subsequently to 1,150. From November 1850, to this day, March 12, 1862, not one single day has been allowed to pass without this contemplated enlargement being brought before God in prayer, and generally more than once a day."

He continued: "Observe then how long it may be before

a full answer to our prayers, even to thousands and tens of thousands of prayers, is granted. I did without the least doubt and wavering look for more than eleven years for the full answer."

Neither did the Lord desire the work to stop after the third house. After the first house was finished, a balance of 776 pounds remained in the building fund along with 500 pounds for current expenses. When the second house was completed, the available balance for expenses was 2,292 pounds. After the last house was finished, the balance on hand for current expenses was 10,309 pounds.

These amounts do not include the money required to carry on the work of the Scriptural Institution, whose expenses came to thousands of pounds each year. All the money needed for these endeavors was brought in through prayer alone.

"As in the case of No. 2," George notes, "so also in the case of the New Orphan House No. 3, I had daily prayed for the needed helpers and assistants for the various departments. Before a stone was laid, I began to pray for this, and as the building progressed, I continued day by day to bring the matter before God."

Before the third house was finished, George experienced much pressure to make it larger than planned. Hundreds of applications had come in since its beginning, so he decided to increase the building's size to accommodate an additional 850 orphans, bringing the total to 2000.

George believed God wanted him to increase his ability to trust Him in faith by taking this new step in his spiritual calling. Once he knew a course of action was God's will, he proceeded quickly to carry it out.

George knew but one course of action—to trust daily for supplies and believe daily for building funds. And this hand to mouth existence—from God's hand to George's and the orphans' mouths—had been so sufficient for the long years past that George did not hesitate to step forth again on a new venture that would shortly provide for almost twice as many children as he then housed.

twelve

George desired to be a greater witness for Christ. When he had housed 1,150 orphans, he wanted to be able to broadcast to the world that God could supply the necessary funds for 2,000. This number became his new prayer goal, and no sooner had the children moved into the third house than George envisioned two more houses—dreams that would gradually come to pass.

Between moving into the second and third houses and beginning construction of the fourth house—a period of four years—George prayed continually that God would supply the money for the new building. He also had to ask God for daily food. But Elijah's God was also George Müller's God, and He heard the cries and petitions of His child.

In small matters as well as big ones, George petitioned the Lord. When workers were hard to find or proved unsuitable, George asked God to furnish the right ones. "Instead of praying once a day about this matter, as we had been doing day by day for years," George recounted, "we met daily three times to bring this before God."

He found no detail too insignificant to take to the Lord in prayer. He literally lived according to the passage, "In every thing by prayer and supplication with thanksgiving let your requests be made known unto God" (Philippians 4:6). George took every need to His heavenly Father: food, shelter, suitable teachers and assistants (these last items were especially important to him). And when details called for attention, they were also subjects of prayer. For instance, when it became difficult to find desirable places for the older boys to work during the summer of 1862, George carried this petition to the Father's throne.

As he explained, "We had several boys ready to be apprenticed; but there were no applications made by masters for apprentices. If all other difficulties were out of the way, the master must also be willing to receive the apprentice into his own family. Under these circumstances, we again gave ourselves to prayer, as we had done for more than twenty years before, concerning this thing. We remembered how good the Lord has been to us in having helped us hundreds of times before in this matter. The difficulty was entirely overcome by prayer, as every one of the boys, whom it was desirable to send out, has been sent out."

In addition to the daily care for the homes with their various needs, George continued to pray that God would enlarge the work. New applications arrived in a never-ending stream, and he could not easily say, "There is no more room."

The desired enlargement of the work would cost at least 50,000 pounds and would increase the current expense fund from $100,000 to $175,000 a year. Nevertheless, George said, "My hope is in God, and in Him alone. I am not a fanatic or enthusiast but, as all who know me are well aware, a calm, cool, quiet, calculating business man; and therefore I should be utterly overwhelmed, looking at it naturally. But as the whole of this work was commenced, and ever has been gone on with, in faith so it is also regarding this enlargement. I look to the Lord alone for helpers, land, means and everything else needed. I have pondered the difficulties for months and have looked steadily at every one of them; but faith in God has put them aside."

Children desiring admission seemed to appear in every direction, and George believed that "the Father of the fatherless" would not turn a deaf ear to his prayer to shelter them. He was again moved with the idea of proving more fully to the world that "the living God is still, as found a thousand years ago, the living God."

All over the world, hundreds of thousands of people had learned of George Müller's work, and many of them had their faith strengthened to undertake greater things in the name of the living God because George had shown them that God was able. His supreme desire was that God might be honored and souls brought into the kingdom. When he became certain that God willed the new step, he decided to go forward at once.

"Many and great may be the difficulties," noted George, "and thousands and tens of thousands of prayers may have to ascend to God before the full answer is obtained. Much exercise of faith and patience may be required; but in the end it will again be seen that His servant, who trusted in Him, has not been confounded."

George wrote about one of the severe trials through

which he passed in 1854: "During the past year my faith was tried in a way it had never been before. My beloved daughter, my only child and a believer for several years, became ill. The illness turned to typhus, and there seemed to be no hope for her recovery. But faith triumphed. My beloved wife and I gave her into the hands of the Lord, and He sustained us both. My soul was in perfect peace, trusting my heavenly Father. She remained very ill for more than two weeks before she began to grow stronger and was moved to Clevedon to recover."

He continued, "Of all the trials of faith I have passed through, this was the greatest. By God's abundant mercy, I was able to delight myself in God, and He gave me the desire of my heart. God is always faithful to those who trust in Him."

The first donations for the fourth house arrived before orphans had moved into the third house and consisted of five rupees, six annas, three senams, three Spanish coins, and three other silver coins. The coins came on June 6, 1861, and a month later, George found a check for two thousand pounds at his house from a friend, who was "thankful to God for the privilege of being a fellow-helper in the work of caring for the orphans."

The gifts came in slowly during the first year or so, but George's faith did not waver. He knew that God, in His own good time, would supply all the necessary funds: "I continue in believing prayer. I have not been allowed to have a shadow of doubt as to whether God can and will give me the means; but day by day, in the full assurance of faith, I renew my requests before God; and generally day by day the amount of the building fund is increased. I then give thanks and ask for more."

After receiving a gift of five thousand pounds on October 3, George believed the time was right to look for some new property. Across the road from the present buildings were eighteen acres of land for which he had been praying. "My eyes had been for years directed to a beautiful piece of land," he recorded. "Hundreds of times had I prayed, within recent years, that God would count me worthy to be allowed to erect on this ground two more Orphan Houses. I might have bought it years ago, but that would have been going before the Lord. I had money enough in hand to have paid for it, but I desired patiently, submissively, to wait God's own time, and for Him to mark it clearly and distinctly that His time was come."

The price had been extremely high throughout the years, but when God was ready for George to take this new step of faith, the owner sold the land for $7,500 less than he originally asked.

In March 1866, with a building fund of 34,002 pounds on hand, George found that construction prices had risen, and it would take approximately 7,000 pounds more to finish the work than he had estimated. He soon realized that the Lord allowed this handicap, for on deeper study and prayer, he decided it would be better to build two houses than one. So he did not sign the contract for building the fourth house, trusting that God would provide the needed funds for both houses. He wrote at the time, "I will not sign contracts, which I had not money in hand to meet. Should it be said that 'God has not money to pay for His own work.'"

As with the earlier buildings, the window glass was donated for the new houses. Ten thousand pounds were needed to furnish the buildings, which came as a result of George's prayers. In February 1868, he announced that all necessary funds were in hand. After waiting on God daily—often several times a day—for nearly seven years, the end of his prayer came at last, and George praised the Lord for once again "filling his mouth" after he had opened it wider than ever before. The total sum required for the two buildings reached the staggering amount of fifty-eight thousand pounds.

After the fourth house opened on November 5, 1868, it still required a tremendous amount of work: transferring children from one house to another, filling in vacancies, and selecting suitable children from hundreds of applications. George declared concerning this venture: "In the mighty monument of prayer raised there was afforded not merely a Christian home for 2,050 destitute orphan children—great indeed as that was—but a supreme and striking object-lesson in simple, child-like faith, a signal evidence of Christ's power and love, sufficient to make men pause, and wonder, and enquire, and—God grant it more and more—believe."

George subordinated everything to the one purpose of demonstrating the fact that God still hears prayer. He believed that he was a public steward of God's property, and he hesitated to spend even a penny needlessly. He constructed the buildings simply and plainly for the orphans' benefit, recognizing that they would likely go to work in similar surroundings. He wanted them to be content with the necessities of life.

Cleanliness, neatness, and order were in evidence

everywhere about the buildings and the grounds. The tracts of land adjoining the buildings were set apart as gardens where the children did their work and exercise. Throughout the houses, everything was neatly arranged. Each child had a numbered compartment for clothes. Each of the boys had three suits, and each girl had five dresses.

With such a large family to supervise, George laid out the orphanages' daily life with regularity and clock-work precision! The children got up at six, and at seven, they were ready for their pre-breakfast duties. Breakfast was at eight, followed by thirty minutes for service before school began at ten. Dinner at one, led up to an afternoon of school work. After school, the children exercised for an hour and a half. Supper was served at six o'clock. George asked the Lord for simple, yet nutritious food such as bread, oatmeal, milk, soups, rice, meat, and vegetables.

In all his building, George said that he sought one end: "We aim at this: that if any of the children do not turn out well, temporally or spiritually, and do not become useful members of society, it shall not at least be our fault."

The expenses continued to increase. But George's faith held strong. On May 26, 1861, he wrote, "At the close of the period I find that the total expenditure for all the various objects was 24,700 pounds, or 67 pounds, 13s, 5 3/4d. per day, all year around. During the coming year I expect the expenses to be considerably greater. But God, who has helped me these many years, will, I believe, help me in the future also. He never failed us."

Year by year, George dutifully recorded this increase of needs followed by God supplying everything. George wrote on July 28, 1874, "It had for months appeared to me, as if the Lord meant to bring us back to the state of things in which we were for more than ten years, from August 1838 until April 1849, when we had day by day, almost without interruption, to look to Him for our daily supplies, and for a great part of the time, from meal to meal. The difficulties appeared to me indeed very great, as the Institution is now twenty times larger than it was then, and our purchases are to be made in a wholesale way; but I am comforted by the knowledge that God is aware of all this. The funds were thus expended; but God, our infinitely rich Treasurer, remains to us. It is this which give me peace."

During all these years, George's faithful wife, Mary, stood with him through the trials and the triumphs of faith. They prayed together side by side, taking hold of God's promises together. But she was not permitted to remain by his side till the end. Mary lived just one month after the opening of the fifth orphan house.

Sadly, George wrote of her death: "Feb. 6, 1870. On Oct. 7, 1830, the Lord gave me my most valuable, lovely, and holy wife. Her value to me and the blessing God made her to be to me is beyond description. This blessing was continued to me till this day, when in the afternoon, about four o'clock, the Lord took her to Himself."

The funeral took place on February 11, with many thousands of people in attendance, including orphans who walked behind the procession. Of the occasion, George said, "I myself, sustained by the Lord to the utmost, performed the service in the chapel, in the cemetery, etc. Shortly after the funeral I was very unwell, but as soon as I was sufficiently recovered, I preached my late dear wife's funeral sermon."

His sermon consisted of a text from Psalm 119:68: "Thou art good, and doest good." As he preached, George drew a picture of a sweet and simple life, made dearer through holy service. He described his wife as "the mother of the orphans." He said, "Every day I miss her more and more. Every day I see more and more how great is her loss to the orphans. Yet without an effort, my inmost soul habitually joys in the joy of the loved departed one. God alone has done it; we are satisfied with Him."

Sixteen months after Mary's death, Mr. James Wright married George's daughter, Lydia. George designated him to be his successor in case of his death. When Mr. Wright accepted this responsibility, George noted: " By the Lord's kindness I am able to work as heretofore. Yet, as I am sixty-six years of age, I cannot conceal from myself that it is of great importance for the work that I should obtain a measure of relief. On this account, I have therefore not only appointed Mr. Wright as my successor, in the event of my death, but have also associated him at present with me in the direction of the Institution."

Another landmark day for George took place fourteen days after his daughter's marriage to James Wright. On that day, he married Susannah Grace Sangar. He had been lonely and restless since Mary's death, and after Lydia's marriage, earnestly desired another companion. Since he and Susannah had known each other for twenty-five years, and she already shared in the orphanage stewardship, she proved to be the Lord's choice for him. Their marriage lasted for twenty-three years, and when God took his second wife home, George also preached her funeral sermon.

But God still had more far-reaching plans for George Müller. Once James Wright was installed as director of the orphanages, George became fairly free of the intense responsibility he had felt for years. Yet his life was far from over. A new journey lay ahead of him, and he was about to embark on the most strenuous years of his life.

thirteen

The way suddenly opened for George to fulfill his life-
long dream of being a missionary. With his new freedom, he would be able to travel the world with God's
message of trust. The idea of telling people on distant mission fields about God's love and faithfulness in response to
prayer thrilled his soul.

Finally, I can go to the mission field! he thought. *I've
wanted to for so many years. How good the Lord is to give
me the desires of my heart. I can tell others what He's done
for me in answer to prayer, He'll do for you. God is no
respecter of persons.*

In his seventieth year, George, like Moses before him,
was about to go forth on an uncharted journey. However,
God knew He could trust George. He had groomed him and
trained him in the school of prayer—but the training had
been connected with the orphanages and their needs. He
had already been a missionary of sorts through the distribution of thousands of Bibles and millions of tracts by the
Institution.

In 1874, Susannah became ill, and George decided to take her to the Isle of Wight for a rest. While there, he preached for a friend, himself a seasoned minister. The preacher told George after the message, "This is the happiest day of my life." The message had stirred him to the depths.

As he thought about this remark, George realized that he could no longer confine his ministry to Bristol. For forty-three years, he had been faithful in the place to which God had called him. But now he felt that God would have him travel from city to city, country to country, to benefit both the Church and the world through his experience of trusting God in faith and prayer.

After seeking the Lord many days in prayer, George laid down seven motives which led him to undertake this worldwide mission:

1. to preach the gospel in its simplicity;
2. to lead believers to know their converted state and realize their privileges in God;
3. to bring believers back to the Bible;
4. to promote among Christians a spirit of brotherly love;
5. to strengthen true Christians, through example of how God had answered his prayers;
6. to promote separateness from the world, as was illustrated in his founding the institution;
7. to fix in the minds of Christians the hope of Christ's coming.

Beginning on March 26, 1875, George began a series of seventeen missionary tours that would take him to forty-two nations, covering two hundred thousand miles by land and water. He preached thousands of times, and from his own estimate during these tours, he spoke to three million people. A friend wrote of these journeys: "The whole of the heavy expenses of these tours was supplied, as in the case of all his other wants, simply and solely in answer to believing prayers."

Further, according to this friend, "George had previously made two tours to Germany in the interest of Christian work while the orphanage was small, but his important life career of missions had its commencement on March 26, in his seventieth year. It was not a long trip, though he terms it 'the beginning of my missionary tours.'"

George continued his travels from Bristol to Brighton, and then, to Sunderland. While on his way to Sunderland, he spoke at the Metropolitan Tabernacle, where Charles Spurgeon pastored. Other leading places where he preached included the Mildmay Park Conference and Edinburgh Castle. After ten weeks, on June 5, the tour closed, but not before George had delivered seventy addresses.

Less than six weeks later, on August 14, 1875, George began his second tour, with Susannah accompanying him. This time, George desired to follow up the revival started by the American evangelists, D. L. Moody and Ira Sankey. He felt that the evangelists' short visits to the various cities did not give the converts time to be led to the higher attainments of grace, and he wanted to use his messages toward this goal.

So he addressed many large audiences in London,

Glasgow, Dublin, and Liverpool, as well as in smaller places. In some cities, especially at Dundee, Glasgow, Liverpool, and Dublin, his audiences numbered from two thousand to six thousand. The tour lasted nearly eleven months, and when it closed in July 1876, he had preached 306 times, an average of one sermon a day. The success of these meetings proved to be so great that George received hundreds of invitations which he could not accept.

When someone asked him later about the results of these missionary trips, he replied: "The day of the Lord alone will reveal it. Here on earth, but little can be known, comparatively, of the fruit of our labors; yet as far as I have been permitted to see, even here, there is good reason to believe that I have not been directed to one single place regarding which there was not manifest proof that the Lord sent me there."

His third tour took him to Europe. It began in August 1876 and ended in June the following year. This tour included Paris, as well as various places in Switzerland, Prussia, Holland, and Alsace.

At Stuttgart, Germany, George held an interview with the Queen of Wurtemberg, who asked him numerous questions about the orphanage in Bristol. By request, at Darmstadt, he spoke in the drawing room of the court preacher. Also present at this meeting were the mother of Prince Louis of Hesse and other princes and princesses. When he preached later in Berlin, the cousin of Chancellor Otto Bismarck traveled 125 miles to hear the person whose book had been a blessing to his spiritual life.

While at his old university town of Halle, George delivered two messages in Francke's Orphan Institution, which had provided the inspiration for his own orphanages. Near Nimenguen, Holland, he also visited an orphanage for 450 children. This orphanage had been begun in total dependence upon God, but its founder had been led because of George's success at the Ashley Down orphanage.

George rejoiced in this and similar undertakings. As he remarked: "Very many Orphan Institutions have been begun in various parts of the world, the founders being encouraged through what God has done for us in Bristol. His Name be magnified."

When this continental tour closed, George received more than sixty written invitations that he could not accept. Through his writings, George had become as well known on the Continent as in England—and abroad, in America.

Thus, his fourth tour took him to the United States and Canada, in response to the numerous invitations he had received from these countries. He believed it to be God's will that he carry the message of faith and trust across the seas. From August 1877 to July of the following year, he traveled throughout Canada and the United States.

George landed in Quebec, where he had his first engagement. Then he traveled down the Atlantic seaboard, speaking in major American cities. From there, he crossed the nation to the Pacific Coast and returned by way of Salt Lake City and back again to New York City. For ten months he blanketed this vast area with his spiritual life messages and crowded the largest auditoriums to capacity.

He spoke to various ethnic groups such as Germans and Scandinavians, and in the South, he spoke to blacks. In addition, many preachers' meetings were organized where his message was directed to the ministers of the people. These meetings gave George greater pleasure than any others. He also relished the theological seminary and university meetings. He knew that in these meetings he was sowing the seeds of his doctrine of trust in fertile minds that would later spread the truth to their growing congregations. Various denominations and Sunday school conventions also allowed him to speak to them.

In Brooklyn, George preached at Dr. Talmage's Tabernacle. Here, he received a warm welcome as he addressed many of the nation's leaders. Through an appointment from the White House, he was received by President and Mrs. Rutherford B. Hayes, who asked about the success of his orphanage work. The tour finished in July 1878, during which he had spoken 308 times and traveled 19,274 miles.

On returning to Bristol, George clarified his purpose: "It is important that I state that my preaching tour in the United States was not set about for the purpose of collecting money for the Institution but only that by my experience and knowledge of Divine things, I might benefit Christians. And that I might preach the Gospel to those who knew not the Lord. The donations handed me for the Institution would not meet one half of its average expenses for one single day."

When they returned to Bristol, the Müllers decided to remain for several weeks and rest. But on September 5, 1878, they set off on their fifth missionary journey in a visit to the Continent. George preached to crowds in English, German, and French. In Spain and Italy, he spoke through an interpreter, not being familiar with the languages. Many doors opened to him among the poor, but in some places, such as in the Riviera, he savored having wealthy and aristocratic people in his audience.

At Barcelona, Spain, George visited ten of the day schools that were entirely supported by the Scriptural Knowledge Institution, and at Madrid he spoke to five schools also dependent on the Institution. He spoke in Rome and Naples, and then visited Vesuvius. As he looked down into the crater, George exclaimed, "What cannot God do!"

While in Italy, he also visited the Vaudois Valley, where so many martyrs had laid down their lives for Christ's sake, and he was deeply moved to accomplish more for his Master than ever before.

Coming back to Bristol on June 18, 1879, George had been gone 9 months and 12 days and had preached 286 times in 46 towns and cities of several nations. However, when he had been in Bristol for 10 weeks, George felt a strong call to visit America once more. So in August, the Müllers set sail for the United States and Canada on their sixth journey. They were gone until June 1880, when George sensed he should return to Bristol. He wanted to relieve the Wrights at the orphanage so they could take a much-needed rest. He had visited 42 different places and had spoken 299 times. In Bristol, he found 154 written invitations which he had not been able to accept.

As he prayed over the invitations, George decided he should take another journey to America in order to stir up the embers of faith. On September 15, 1880, he and his wife returned to the United States by way of Canada and stayed until the end of May 1881. They spent three months in New York alone where he preached 93 meetings, 38 of which were in German. During this visit he spoke 250 times altogether.

The weather was severe in New York that winter, and considering that he was seventy-five, George's labors were incredible. Concerning her husband, Susannah Müller wrote: "That winter was the coldest that has been known in New York for thirty years, and the many long drives my beloved husband took at night when the weather was most severe, were very trying. Constrained by the love of Christ, however, he persevered in a service that would have been considered, by most persons of his age, an arduous undertaking.

The Müllers returned to Bristol where George again relieved the Wrights. After being in Bristol for eight weeks, George sensed a strong desire to visit missionaries in the East. On August 23, 1881, they left for the European Continent once more, and George spoke in Germany and in Switzerland.

From there, the Müllers traveled to Alexandria, Cairo, Port Said, and on to the Holy Land. George reveled in visiting the many places where Jesus had lived and walked. They went to Gethsemane and Golgotha, the Mount of Olives and Bethany, Bethlehem and Jerusalem. Leaving the Holy Land, the Müllers journeyed to Constantinople, Athens, Rome, and Florence. George preached in English and German on this tour, and used an interpreter when the people he was addressing spoke Arabic, Armenian, Turkish, or Greek.

After resting briefly in Bristol, George undertook his ninth journey on August 8, 1882. This tour extended until June 1, 1883. George went to Germany, Austria, Hungary, Bohemia, Russia, and Poland. The trip's highlight came when he preached at Kroppenstaedt, his birthplace, after a sixty-four-year absence. Here he was asked to give his life story to a capacity crowd in the city's largest building.

In Russia, George was a guest of Princess Lieven and spoke in St. Petersburg. Leaving Russia, he traveled to Poland and spoke at Lodz. A touching incident involved a letter of invitation signed by most of the populace: they urged George to stay longer.

By this time, George had "itching feet," and after a short respite in Bristol, he desired to see the Orient—and fulfill a life-long dream of being a missionary in the Far East. So on September 26, 1883, his tenth tour began. Almost sixty years earlier he had hoped to be a missionary to the East Indies, and now the Lord was allowing him to carry out this ambition in a new way. India would be the twenty-third country visited in George's tours.

George traveled more than twenty-one thousand miles and spoke two hundred times to missionaries, Christian workers, European residents, and the nationals. He was delighted to see the orphanage at Colar. He knew that in this his seventy-ninth year, God had graciously blessed him. God used this tour to quicken the spiritual life of the missionaries and to awaken the national workers to their need of a life of full dependence upon God.

After returning to Bristol for a short time, George was off on yet another tour. He made two brief tours—one to South Wales, the other to the Lake District, Dundee (Scotland), and Liverpool.

In November 1885, when George was eighty years old, he left on another long missionary journey to Australia,

China, Japan, and the Straits of Malacca. He desired especially to establish and encourage the Chinese missionaries in their difficult struggles. In Japan he held mass meetings. At one Japanese gathering, more than twenty-five hundred Japanese heard him speak through an interpreter.

George had been gone from Bristol for eighteen months, and when he returned, he had traveled 37,280 miles, preaching wherever he could. George's strength seemed limitless on these journeys. God had given him abundant-life energy, enabling him to tell the world that this blessing could be theirs as well.

After staying in Bristol for two months, George set out on yet another journey. He was eighty-two years old and would travel this time to South Australia, Tasmania, New Zealand, Ceylon, and India. This tour lasted twelve months and was greatly used of the Lord to strengthen the faith of believers wherever George spoke. Rejoicing over the results, George said, "Believers were edified, and the unconverted persons brought through my ministry to a knowledge of the Lord."

In India he preached to large audiences of nationals who appeared caught up in his words. However, the intensely hot weather of Ceylon and India were difficult for George to bear, and people tried to tell him he was working too hard for a man of his age. In Calcutta, the heat proved so suffocating that he decided to follow the medical advice to leave. On the way to Darjeeling, he thought he was going to die. But a short rest helped him to recuperate and continue on with his tour.

George received some devastating news at Jubbulpore

when James Wright cabled that his daughter, Lydia, had died. She had worked without compensation in the orphan houses for thirty out of her fifty-eight years. At the news, George hastened back to Bristol.

"My heart," George admitted, "remained in perfect peace because I took this affliction, as I had taken former heavy trials, out of the hand of my heavenly Father, fully realizing that He had taken her to Himself and had done therefore the very best thing that could happen, and that to me this event would work for my good."

After being in Bristol at Ashley Down for four months, George left to travel to the Continent for Susannah's health. This trip turned into another missionary journey, his sixteenth, as he spoke to crowded assemblies every place he went.

About this trip he noted: "My heart has been greatly refreshed at seeing almost everywhere in Germany and Switzerland such a desire to hear the truth, notwithstanding the departure of so many persons from it."

Following this trip, the Müllers returned to Bristol for a short time. Then George's recurring burden to preach what God had taught him persuaded him to travel again. He was eighty-six years old, and he traveled to Germany, Holland, Austria, and Italy. When this twelve months' journey ended in May 1892, it proved to be his last.

God had granted George amazing grace, enabling him to start his missionary journeys at seventy years of age and continue them unabated for seventeen years. He had traveled hundreds of thousands of miles, preaching between six and eight thousand times outside his home city of Bristol to more than three million people.

Even to the end of his life he spoke with vigor. Someone tells of a sermon George preached in Berlin when he was eighty-six. He urged believers never to yield to discouragement, pointing out that it was their spiritual duty to seek the deep secret of rest for their souls. "Saved believers," George declared, "can know their position in the Lord. You must become acquainted with the Scriptures, the hope of your salvation." He stressed that God alone is the satisfying portion of the soul.

Throughout these missionary tours, every need was miraculously supplied. The tremendous cost of steamer and train fares, as well as hotel accommodations, was always on hand as the Lord sent it.

Frequently people asked George why he did not stay at home and supervise the work for the Ashley Down Houses. He replied that under Mr. Wright's supervision, the needs of the houses were met. Further, he noted that it was not necessary for him to be at home to oversee the needs. Believing that his presence was needed was a contradiction of the very principles upon which the work was started. "Real trust in God is above circumstances and appearances," he insisted.

To confirm his views, during the third year of his missionary journeys, the income for the Scriptural Knowledge Institution was larger than it had ever been during the previous forty-four years of its existence.

George enjoyed the seventeen years of missionary journeys tremendously. He considered them the richest and ripest years he had ever had. "Very godly and advanced

Christians have told me," he stressed about his endeavors, "that they consider my present labors the most important of my whole life."

fourteen

George Müller's name has most often been associated with orphanage work—especially in the city of Bristol, England. Indeed, this part of his life's work has been so highlighted as to diminish his other achievements. He was well received on his seventeen missionary tours because the world considered him the orphan's friend. His message consisted of faith and trust, and George drew illustrations from his experiences caring for thousands of orphans simply through prayer.

Another facet of his life's work resided in the Scriptural Knowledge Institution. When he founded the Institution on February 20, 1834, he wrote: "I trust this matter is of God." Through the institution he desired to distribute Bibles, tracts, and other Christian materials.

Being a worthy steward of God's resources always played the uppermost role in George's life. The Scriptural Knowledge Institution began quietly and without fanfare. A few people had gathered to consider a work that should assist Sunday schools as well as day schools where the teachers were Christian, distribute Bibles and religious tracts, and care for orphans.

Of course, George considered the orphanage work as the last of the Institution's goals in the beginning. But it grew to overshadow the other aspects of the Institution's aims. The orphans and their care required much of his overall energy in time and prayer. However, God certainly allowed this development and was pleased with it.

The Institution began with God as its Patron and never veered from this original plan. George believed that God meant what He said when affirming "the silver and the gold are mine." If the work was truly of God, He would provide adequate silver and gold to promote it.

Someone wrote concerning the Institution's work: "The Lord was the Banker of the Institution. He knew all would be well. Slowly but surely the little institution grew. Faith and its heavenly response went hand in hand, and being weighted and borned down by no anxiety as to debt, as many religious agencies are, the trustful founder was able to give himself wholly to prayer for the means and grace to carry the work on."

The Institution's first report covered its first fifteen months. Although not an outstanding report, it was the spring from which a mighty river of influence would go forth to water the earth's harvest fields. George could report: "It is now fifteen months since, in dependence upon the Lord for the supply of means, we have been enabled to supply poor children with schooling, circulate the Holy Scriptures, and aid missionary labors. During this time, though the field of labor has been continually enlarged, and though we have been brought low in funds, the Lord has never allowed us to be obliged to stop the work. We have been enabled during this time to establish three day schools, and to connect with the Institution two other charity day schools."

He went on to note: "In addition to this the expenses connected with a Sunday school and an Adult school have been likewise defrayed, making seven schools altogether. The number of children that have thus been provided with school, in the day schools alone amounts to 439. The number of copies of the Holy Scriptures which have been circulated is 795 Bibles and 753 New Testaments. We have also sent, in aid of Missionary labors in Canada, in the East Indies and on the Continent of Europe, 117 pounds, 11s." Clearly, George was pleased with the Institution's direction.

Each year God wondrously supplied the needs of the Institution in response to George's prayers. The report of 1855 showed that more than 7,204 pounds had been given to the support of schools for the previous twenty-one years, and another 16,115 pounds had been donated for missions. A total of 13,949 Bibles and 9,047 New Testaments had been distributed at a cost of 3,389 pounds during the same period.

That year, George reported, "Without any one having been personally applied to for anything by me the sum of 74,132 pounds was given to me for the orphans as a result of prayer to God from the commencement of the work up to May 26, 1855."

Throughout the years, God took care of every need. In the Fifty-fourth Report of the Institution for the year 1893 (the fifty-ninth year of the work), George wrote: "The readers of the last report will remember under what particular trials we entered upon the last financial year of the Institution but we trusted in God, and with unshaken confidence in Him, and expected that we should somehow or the other be helped. While thus we went on, my heart at peace habitually, being assured that all this was permitted by God, to prepare a blessing for thousands, who would afterward read the record of His dealings with us from May 26, 1892, to May 26, 1893."

During that year of trial, the Lord spoke to George as he again read Psalm 81:10, "Open thy mouth wide, and I will fill it."

"Remembering the work of the Holy Spirit in my heart when reading this verse on December 5, 1835, and the effect which this had in leading me to found the greatest Orphan Institution in the world. . . ," George recorded, "putting the Bible aside I fell on my knees and asked God that He would graciously be pleased to repeat His former kindness, and to supply me again more abundantly with means. Accordingly in less than half an hour, I received 50 pounds from a Bristol donor. By the last delivery, at 9:00 P.M., I had 152 pounds in all, this day, as the result of prayer."

In the last Report of the Institution that George ever gave (for the year 1896-97), he gave a detailed summary of the blessings of God upon the work since its founding. "This is the last record," someone has written, "which Mr. Müller penned of his stewardship, and he was fully assured that the fruit which he had been enabled to see was but little in comparison with what he should behold in the day of Christ's appearing."

This incredible final report shows how amply God responded to George's prayers. The report noted 121,683 pupils

141

in the schools. And George rejoiced in Bible distribution: "During the past 63 years there have been circulated by means of this Institution, in almost all parts of the world, and in many different languages, 281,652 Bibles, 1,448,662 New Testaments, 21,343 copies of the Book of Psalms, and 222,196 other portions of the Holy Scriptures. On this branch of the Institution the Lord's blessing has been asked day by day for sixty-three years; and the Lord has blessed this work most abundantly." The Scriptures had gone as missionaries all over the world: England, Ireland, Scotland, Spain, Australia, and numerous other countries—even to obscure villages.

George mentioned two countries formerly closed to the Scriptures and Christian work and the blessing of Bible distribution there: "When it pleased God to open Spain, in the year 1868, I sought at once with thousands, yea, many thousands of copies, of the Holy Scriptures to enter into Spain; and it pleased God most abundantly to bless the simple reading of the Holy Scriptures in Spanish (which they had never seen in their whole life) to multitudes.

"And when Italy was opened for the preaching of the Truth and the circulation of the Holy Scriptures, it pleased the Lord to grant to me the great privilege to enter immediately into Italy with the Italian Bible and New Testament, in thousands of copies, and they were spread in all directions; and, in answer to our prayers, most abundantly were they blessed." The Bibles were sent into numerous countries in answer to prayer. God richly supplied the resources and blessed the distribution efforts.

George gave glowing reports in this last record of the

other goals of the Institution: missionary operations, tract distribution, and the orphan work. Last, he recorded the money received to carry out the work.

When he reviewed the previous sixty-one years of the orphan work, George noted that it had been singularly blessed of God. He rejoiced that 2,813 orphans "left the Institution as believers." In addition, "We had information by letter or other means that many hundreds were brought to the knowledge of the Lord after they had left the Institution." He also answered objections to those who said the conversions would not last: "My reply is, 50 or 60 years ago a number of young orphans professed faith in the Lord Jesus, and, with a few exceptions, they walked in the fear of God, 20, 30, 40 years, till the Lord took them to Himself."

As George totaled the finances the Lord had provided for the Institution's various projects from its inception on March 5, 1834, until 1897, he was overwhelmed. "The total amount of money received, by prayer and faith, for the various objects of the Institution during the past sixty-one years is one million four hundred and twenty-four thousand six hundred and forty-six pounds, six shillings and ninepence (1,424,646 pounds, 6s)."

The Lord grandly rewarded George's faith, for in response to his prayers approximately seven and a half million dollars came in for the work. From a most insignificant beginning, the work grew until it became a leading supporter of missions and distributor of Bibles and religious literature. And George Müller became known worldwide as the outstanding "father of the orphans."

George took to heart the Lord's commission to him to

be a "father of the orphans," and the success of the orphanage work reverberated in mission circles worldwide. But the Institution's work in distributing Bibles and Christian materials along with missionary aid was also considerable. Thus, George's life was one of dual service—founder of the Institution and of the orphanage.

fifteen

The building of George's spiritual life reveals constant conflict. On the outside he showed a calm attitude toward circumstances, yet inwardly he battled to obtain this seeming peace. His battles were more intense during the earliest years of his faith pilgrimage and came upon him more frequently to block his climb toward spiritual serenity. However, George would always face obstacles that hindered his communion with God.

Lack of prayer appears more evident during the years just after his conversion. Like anyone else, George realized a habit of prayer must be built by diligence. He didn't achieve it overnight. When he was a student at Halle, just after his conversion, he decided to leave for the University of Berlin. But the Spirit checked him at once for not praying about it first. George admitted, "When the morning came on which I had to apply to the university for testimonials, the Lord graciously stirred me up prayerfully to consider the matter."

After he prayed about the matter, he discovered it was not God's will for him to make the change. This seemingly insignificant incident taught George the importance of praying about everything in his life. Later on, he had many experiences of being checked by the Lord before veering off on a wrong course.

Before undertaking any venture, George remembered the episode at Halle. He undertook any new course of action only after a waiting period of prayer, refusing to act before receiving God's sanction.

Early in 1826, George learned another lesson: Bible reading. Although he was a Christian, he did not read his Bible, though he read books about the Bible extensively. But George needed to master the lesson of regular Bible reading before God trusted him with many answers to prayer.

Of those days, George confessed, "My difficulty in understanding the Bible, and the little enjoyment I had in reading it, made me careless in reading it."

The statement was true in 1826, but when sixteen years of his spiritual warfare had passed, George discovered a radical change in himself. "Before this time my practice had been at least for ten years previously, as an habitual thing to give myself to prayer after having dressed myself in the morning. Now I saw that the most important thing I had to do was to give myself to the reading of the Word of God, and to meditation on it, that my heart might be comforted, encouraged, warned, reproved."

After having first prepared his heart through reading the Bible, George would begin his prayer time. Of these times, he admitted, "The result is that there is always a good deal of confession."

When the London Society accepted him as a missionary,

one of the conditions was that he would study with them for six months. This ultimatum brought him great disappointment. In 1828, George acknowledged that "for a few moments, therefore, I was greatly disappointed and tried." He wanted to do something for God—not just study! These trials and discouragements were to be a constant companion throughout his entire Christian life.

Victories of faith were so great in George's life, it's hard to believe he ever had trials or that he was ever disappointed waiting for answers to prayer. Nevertheless he had many trials and experienced much disappointment.

On March 7, 1831, he wrote, "I was again tempted to disbelieve the faithfulness of the Lord, and though I was not miserable, still, I was not so fully resting upon the Lord that I could triumph with joy." He had dire need, and it seemed that God had forgotten him. Shortly however, his disappointment turned to joy when the answer came.

Seven years later this same trial overwhelmed him. On September 17, 1838, he wrote, "This evening I was rather tried respecting the long delay of larger sums coming." The next year George wrote of "the trials of faith during the year," but added, "Should it be supposed. . .by anyone in reading the details of our trials of faith during the year. . .that we have been disappointed in our expectations or discouraged in the work, my answer is. . .such days were expected from the commencement. Our desire is not that we may be without trials of faith, but that the Lord graciously be pleased to support us in the trial."

George also mentioned "the deeper trials of his faith," those things that really disturbed him and caused his mind to wander during times of meditation. These distractions bothered him regularly.

He found release from these times of conflict by going to his knees in prayer. "When other trials, still greater which I cannot mention, have befallen me," he explained, "I poured out my soul before God, and arose from my knees in peace." Thus he received strength and encouragement as well as peace through prayer.

There were occasions when everything appeared bleak. He confided, "When sometimes all has been dark, exceedingly dark judging from natural appearances; yea, when I should have been overwhelmed indeed in grief and despair had I looked at things after the outward appearances. . .I have sought to encourage myself by laying hold in faith on God's almighty power, His unchangeable love, and His infinite wisdom."

Some years afterward George received a great disappointment when a believer told him that she could not send the large sums she had promised. A short time later, George realized he had put his trust in the promise of the woman and not in the promise of God. The Lord spoke gently to him through the verse, "We know that all things work together for good to them that love God." Immediately peace flooded his distressed soul.

George was concerned that no one who read his "Narrative" or came into contact with God's dealings with him would think that he was immune from spiritual need. He referred to being in constant need more than twenty years after he first began to trust God for his daily supplies. These needs involved more than finances. He knew more immediate freedom from financial worries and victory over his heavy financial burdens than over his other more personal needs.

His temptations came often in the form of appearing insincere or of being proud over what God had done through him. He wrote about the stress of such spiritual problems often arising in his soul: "I am in continual need. If left to myself I should fall a prey to Satan. Pride, unbelief or other sins would be my ruin. I cannot stand for a moment left to myself. O, that none of my readers might think that I could not be puffed up by pride, and think of me as being beyond unbelief. No, I am as weak as ever."

In 1848 he added: "I need as much as ever to be upheld as to faith and every other grace. I am therefore in 'need,' in great 'need,' and therefore, dear Christian readers, help me with your prayers."

To prove to us that he was not above trials, he said, "Straits and difficulties I expected from the beginning. Therefore the longer I go on in this service, the greater the trials of one kind or another become." George had his weak moments like everyone else, and though strong in faith, he still felt the constant urge to keep in constant contact with God. Otherwise, he knew his inner weaknesses would overcome him.

On May 13, 1837, he confessed, "Today I have had again much reason to mourn over my corrupt nature, particularly on account of want of gratitude for the many temporal mercies by which I am surrounded. I was so sinful as to be dissatisfied on account of the dinner. I thought it would not agree with me, instead of thanking God for rich provisions and asking heartily the Lord's rich blessing upon it. I rejoice in the prospect of that day, when, seeing Jesus as He is, I shall be like Him."

George was often troubled by the many spiritual voids that marked his work. When he realized that the Lord was using brother Craik more than himself, for example, he set aside more time for prayer to discover the cause. He felt convicted of a lack of concern for the sinner's welfare, and once he found the root cause, he attempted to remedy it.

Through the years George worried a good deal about his tendency to become irritable because of his physical problems. During the first decade after his conversion he fought to overcome any slight indication that he was not pleased with how he felt, or how the weather might be, or whatever emotional circumstances he was experiencing. He reported on January 16, 1838: "The weather has been cold for several days, but today I suffered much, either because it was colder than before or because I felt it more owing to the weakness of my body. I was a little irritated by this. At last, having prayed for some time, I was obliged to rise and take a walk."

He continued, "I now entreated the Lord that this circumstance might not be permitted to rob me of the precious communion which I had with Him the last three days, for this was the object at which Satan aimed. I confessed also my sin of irritability on account of the cold and sought to have my conscience cleansed through the blood of Jesus. He had mercy upon me, my peace was restored, and I had uninterrupted communion with Him." In 1844, George remarked, "I desired more power over my besetting sins." It is likely the sin of irritability was one of the sins that plagued him regularly.

His entire life was marked with afflictions, irritations, trials, and the victory of peace and spiritual repose. When his daughter, Lydia, came down with typhus fever in 1854, George noted: "Now was the trial of faith. But faith triumphed. While I was in this affliction, this great affliction, besides being at peace as far as the Lord's dispensation was concerned, I also felt perfectly at peace with regard to the cause of the affliction. It was the Father's rod, applied in infinite wisdom and love for the restoration of my soul from a state of lukewarmness. Conscious as I was of my manifold weaknesses, failings and shortcomings, so that I too would be ready to say with the Apostle Paul, 'O wretched man that I am!' yet I was assured that this affliction was for the trial of my faith."

Early in his Christian life, George discovered the route of peace through affliction. As far back as 1829 he wrote, "The weaker I became in body, the happier I was in my spirit." He made this statement during a severe illness on May 15 when he despaired of living.

He went on, "Never in my whole life had I seen myself so vile, so guilty, so altogether what I ought not to have been as at this time. It was as if every sin of which I had been guilty was brought to my remembrance; but at the same time I could realize that all my sins have been completely forgiven. The result of this was great peace."

George gave one of his last reports on March 1, 1898: "For about twenty-one months with scarcely the least intermission the trial of our faith and patience has continued. Now, today, the Lord has refreshed my heart." He rejoiced over receiving a seventy-five hundred dollar legacy.

George had learned the simple lesson that however great the affliction, God in His kind providence would not forsake him—given that he remained steadfast in faith and continued in prayer.

He discovered the key to spiritual victory early in his Christian life. On June 25, 1835, he wrote, "These last three days I have had very little real communion with God, and have therefore been very weak spiritually, and have several times felt irritability of temper." The next day he noted, "I was enabled, by the grace of God, to rise early, and I had nearly two hours in prayer before breakfast. I now feel this morning more comfortable."

George gleaned from his prayer life freedom from doubt, distemper, and the after-effects of a trial. When peace encompassed his soul, he knew the Lord received his prayers. He recorded on March 9, 1847, "The greater the difficulties, the easier for faith." And a little later, "The greater the trial, the sweeter the victory."

He denied having the gift of faith. He had faith, as any Christian may, but not that special gift of which the apostle Paul spoke in 1 Corinthians 12:9.

"Think not that I have the gift of faith which is mentioned along with 'the gifts of healing,' 'the working of miracles' and that on that account I am able to trust in God. If I were only one moment left by myself my faith would utterly fail. It is not true that my faith is that gift of faith. It is the self-same faith which is found in every believer for little by little it has been increasing for the last six and twenty years."

In looking at George Müller's life of trust and the multiplied answers to his prayers, we must be careful not to remove him from the realm of the thoroughly human. He wished for every Christian to see their own possibilities in the area of prayer. George possessed no character traits nor divine possessions not within the reach of every believer.

The trials that blocked his spiritual growth were those common to every Christian. The human tempers, the frailties of his body, mind, and spirit were those which mark true believers in God's kingdom. His victories came through prayer, trust in the Lord's unfailing promises, and faith that God's truth could not fail. He would desire that each Christian see that similar faith victories are also within his reach.

George gave one last word on prayer: "It is not enough to begin to pray, nor to pray aright; nor is it enough to continue for a time to pray; but we must patiently, believingly continue in prayer, until we obtain an answer; and further, we have not only to continue in prayer unto the end, but we have also to believe that God does hear us and will answer our prayers. Most frequently we fail in not continuing in prayer until the blessing is obtained, and in not expecting the blessing."

sixteen

George Müller's entire life revolved around giving. He prayed so that he would be able to give. When he prayed, God provided the necessary supplies, not only for his own family, but also for his larger family of orphans. Because God gave to him through faith, he needed to be among those who were faithful givers.

The Scripture verses that most influenced George had to do with giving and receiving. George wrote these passages across the pages of his book. One of the first texts that impressed both him and his wife was "Sell that ye have, and give alms" (Luke 12:33). This verse threw light on the Müllers' pathway like a beacon and directed the course of their lives.

Another verse that greatly affected George and his devotional life was "Whatsoever ye shall ask in my name, that will I do" (John 14:13). He based his work on this promise and asked of God so that God would be glorified through His provision.

Since God had told George to "open your mouth wide," he never feared he was asking too much. George considered this promise the basis of all spiritual and temporal success. Approaching the Lord bird-like, he opened his mouth, and the Lord filled it, supplying all his needs.

George delighted in the Lord's name that is recorded in Genesis 22:14: Jehovah Jireh, which meant "the Lord will provide." Like Abraham, he knew that when he had a need, the Lord Himself would supply whatever it was.

The earliest records of George's donations show him giving generously. During the first year of his life of trust (1831), he received 151 pounds in answer to prayer, but he gave away 50 pounds of the total amount. The next year, he received 195 pounds and gave away 70 pounds. In 1833 his income (through faith) was 267 pounds, and his gifts came to 110 pounds.

This ratio of receiving and giving corresponded similarly throughout his long life. For the ten years from 1836 to 1845, George's income from all sources was approximately 3,400 pounds, and through faith, he gave back into the Lord's work about 1,280 pounds. During the next ten years, his yearly income was about 500 pounds, and for the same time period, he gave over half of this amount away. His gifts for the ten years came to 2,660 pounds.

The years from 1856 to 1865 yielded an income of 10,670 pounds (over $50,000 a year); and from this amount he gave 8,250 pounds, or a total sum of $41,250, to the Lord's work. Then, from 1866 to 1875, George returned 1,800 pounds a year to Christian concerns. This amount came from a total of 20,500 pounds. During the next ten years, the last record available, George gave away 22,330 pounds out of the entire amount of 26,000 pounds! He was left with 3,670 pounds to live on for a period of ten years, or a little over

$1,800 a year. Since that period was devoted to extensive missionary travels, his personal finances would have been stretched quite a bit.

Whatever donations he received came by faith alone, and George realized he was the channel through which God's gifts would flow out to others in need. He considered himself the Lord's steward, and he believed that whatever money he received should be given rather than hoarded. One of the givers to the orphanage work through the years was a crippled woman. She gave small amounts, but her philosophy of giving matched George's. She began giving a penny a week to the work from her earnings, and the Lord blessed her so much that she was able to raise her weekly gift to six shillings, or a dollar and a half. She wrapped one gift in a piece of paper on which she had written: "Give; give; give—be ever giving. If you are living, you will be giving. Those who are not giving are not living."

The total amount George gave away from his own income from 1831 to November 1877 came to $180,000. This sum came from his own sparse lifestyle. The only money he possessed he prayed in each day.

The Fifty-ninth Report of the Institution, issued May 26, 1898, immediately after George's death, reveals a very interesting item concerning his method of giving. Year by year in the annual reports there were frequent entries of gifts "from a servant of the Lord Jesus, who constrained by the love of Christ, seeks to lay up treasure in heaven."

James Wright, who succeeded George as head of the institution, checked these entries and found that this "servant of the Lord" had given up to March 1, 1898, the total sum of 81,490 pounds, 18 shillings, and 8 pence.

Of course the servant was George himself who gave out of his own money more than 64,500 pounds to the Scriptural Knowledge Institution alone, and to other individuals and organizations 17,000 more. How inconceivable that a man with such limited means should give over $407,450 to the work of God!

When George died, his entire personal estate amounted to 169 pounds, 9s., 4d., or approximately $850, of which his household effects, books, furniture, and other items, represented well over $500. The only cash in his possession was actually about $350. He died a poor man, though the Lord had entrusted to his hands well over a half-million dollars.

Considering himself a steward of God, George sought to live by the verse: "Give, and it shall be given unto you; good measure, pressed down, and shaken together, and running over, shall men give into your bosom" (Luke 6:38).

Believing this verse, he witnessed the Lord giving back to him abundantly. He said, "I had given, and God caused to be given to me again and bountifully." George believed what he read in the Bible. Through acting on God's promises and rejecting the offer of a definite salary of fifty-five pounds a year, George literally received a fortune—a fortune which he shared with those in need.

Giving was to George the heart of the Christian life. Give yourself in full surrender to God, and from what God gives return to Him generous gifts.

George had strong convictions on the subject of giving. He listed some of them: "Many of the children of God lose in a great measure the privilege, and also the blessing to their own souls of communicating to the Lord's work to the necessities of the poor, for want of a regular habit of giving." Responding to the question, "How shall I give?" he stated the following:

1. Seek to keep before you that the Lord Jesus Christ has redeemed us, and that we are not our own, because we are bought with a price. All then that we have belongs to Him, and we have to look on our possessions as a faithful steward.
2. The habitual using of our means, the regularly communicating as the Lord prospers us, is next to be attended to. As far as practicable, we should seek to do this weekly, according to the word—'Upon the first day of the week let every one of you lay by him in store, as God hath prospered him' (1 Corinthians 16:2).
3. Every one should do so. . . .
4. With regard to the amount to be given, no rule can be laid down, because what we ought to do should not be done in a legal spirit, but from love and gratitude to the Blessed One Who died for us.

Some other questions about giving and his responses are:

Q. How shall I put aside my gifts? Must I actually separate this money from my other money?
A. That is the simplest and in many respects the best way. A memorandum book may be kept, in

which on one side is entered what is put aside
for the Lord, to be expended on the poor, or for
other benevolent and religious purposes, and on
the other side may be put down what has been
expended, and from time to time a balance may
be struck. The amount thus put aside for the
Lord is of course faithfully to be used for Him,
else it would be mocking God; and therefore,
instead of obtaining a blessing, it would rather
be a curse.

Q. Am I to give with the idea of being repaid by
the Lord?

A. Though we should never give for the sake of
being repaid by the Lord, still, this will be the
case, if we give from right motives. It is God's
own declaration that it will be so. This is plainly
to be gathered from the following passages:
"Give, and it shall be given unto you". . ."He
that hath pity on the poor, lendeth unto the
Lord; and that which he hath given will He pay
him again."

George also stressed that a Christian's giving must be to the
Lord. Other people may be the recipients, but gifts must be
humbly offered not for the praise of man, but for the blessings of God.

Of course George's own experience and the many letters
he received testified to the blessing associated with system-
atic giving. An Irish manufacturer wrote saying: "I enclose a
Post Office order for 5 pounds, which by the blessing of

Almighty God, I am enabled to send you this year. You will no doubt remember that the first sum I sent to you was 5s. I think that was four years ago; and indeed at that time it was a large sum for me to send.

"For some years previous to the time I sent you the first amount I was at times much perplexed over the subject of giving; and the end of my reasoning was always that a person so straitened in circumstances as I was then, was not called upon to give. I kept this opinion until one of your Reports fell into my hands, and from the accounts contained therein, was encouraged to send you the first amount of 5s. Soon after I thought my circumstances got somewhat easier. I have proved that just as I give the Lord gives in return. I sometimes withheld when I ought not, and just as I withheld, the Lord, in His infinite mercy withheld also. But above all, I have to thank God that my spiritual condition is much improved since I began to give."

Another facet of giving that George insisted upon was obtaining gifts in God's way. "It is not enough to obtain means for the work of God," he said, "but that these means should be obtained in God's way. To ask unbelievers for means is not God's way; to press even believers to give is not God's way; but the duty and the privilege of being allowed to contribute to the work of God should be pointed out, and this should be followed up with earnest prayer, believing prayer, and will result in the desired end." Throughout his life, he maintained this principle.

George also thought that giving in adversity would prove a greater blessing than giving in prosperity. Giving in adversity, when needs were pressing, shows that one truly trusts in

God for supplying daily needs, while giving in prosperity places upon the giver no particular hardship.

George also refused to hoard goods or money. "I have every reason to believe that had I begun to lay up, the Lord would have stopped the supplies," he wrote. "Let no one profess to trust in God, and yet lay up for the future wants, otherwise the Lord will first send him to the hoard he has amassed, before he can answer the prayer for more."

God richly supplied George and his work with donations of every type and description. Money was sent in from nearly every possible source. Some gifts were large, running into the thousands of dollars, and others were but a penny. People sent him gifts of bread and shoes. Some individuals were constrained of the Lord to sell articles of furniture and make a contribution to the orphanage work. Many items of jewelry worth many thousands of dollars were given to George to be sold for the work.

Some of the more unusual gifts came in the form of autographs to be sold. These included the autographs of William IV and Sir Robert Peel. One man sent in a silver medal which he had won in the battle of Java; yet another delivered a horsecar to be sold; and one woman donated her original published hymns for sale.

When needs were extreme, George called the staff together for prayer, and often as they finished praying, dray wagons would be backing up to the kitchen door loaded with buns, bread, apples, cakes, potatoes, boxes of soap, sacks of peas, haunches of venison, rabbits and pheasants, and every other type of food imaginable.

Some of the gifts George recorded in the last year of his

life were: 7,203 quaterns of bread; 5,222 buns, 306 cakes; 44,669 pounds of apples; 40 sacks of potatoes; 20 boxes of soap; 9 tons of coal; 26 haunches of venison; 112 rabbits; 312 pheasants; 5 bags of oatmeal; 26 cases of oranges; 5 boxes of dates; and 4,013 pounds of meat, along with hundreds of other items.

In May 1842, George received a gold watch sent by an anonymous donor. The attached note read: "A pilgrim does not want such a watch as this to make him happy; one of an inferior kind will do to show how swiftly time flies, and how fast he is hastening on to that Canaan where time will be no more."

One man lost half of his property and felt led to send George five hundred dollars as a thank offering because God had spared the other half of his property. A friend sold pickles and earned three dollars which he sent quickly as a gift.

When God provided a fisherman with a good catch of herring one night, he promptly sent George fifteen dollars to be used for the orphanage. One person, after cutting down a tree and selling it, sent the home five pounds, seventeen shillings from the sale of the wood. A little boy found a ring and on delivering it to its rightful owner, received a shilling, which he took to the home as a gift.

Many people gave in response to the blessing of God on their lives and for calamities averted. George received a letter one day with fifteen dollars enclosed. The writer said: "I have never lost an article, although my premises are so situated that they might be easily entered at night, thus showing how the Lord watches over those who trust in Him." The gift represented the money which a watch dog would have cost.

A veterinary surgeon, while attending a sick horse, had given it up for dead, but after praying over the animal, the horse recovered, so the man sent George a gift. Another person, who broke his left arm, sent a small gift in thanks to God that he had not broken his right arm, or some more vital part such as his neck!

The gifts were too many to enumerate, but they were prompted by every possible circumstance. Some people restored thefts committed years earlier. Others thanked God for a happy married life. Thank offerings were contributed by those whose lost or stolen property had been recovered.

Throughout the years the Lord met the needs of the orphans by drawing on thousands of bountiful storehouses that were consecrated to His work. When a need arose, George would pray diligently for it, and soon, either nearby or thousands of miles away, God would drop in someone's heart the desire to send the answer. For over sixty-three years, God lined up every petition prayed with the appropriate gift.

seventeen

W hen his missionary tours ended in May 1892, George Müller spent his energies caring for the Scriptural Knowledge Institution. He assisted James Wright and assumed a large share of the work. Even at eighty-seven, he was energetic and continued to be active in Christian work.

He still looked after the congregation at Bethesda; the congregation had grown from the original seven believers to a membership of more than twelve hundred. George also took turns with others preaching on Sunday mornings to several different congregations. Attending numerous prayer meetings as time permitted appealed to him as well. Sometimes he was invited to speak outside Bristol, though he did not make these opportunities into extended preaching tours as he had done in the past.

An active, happy old man, he derived his pleasure from caring for the Lord's work. But more and more he gave himself to his chief delight—reading the Bible and meditating on it while petitioning the Lord. During his latter years, he read the Bible through four times each year.

In his sermons he spoke with the vigor of a younger man. A. T. Pierson heard him speak on Sunday morning, March 22, 1896, in Bethesda Chapel. George Müller was ninety years old. According to Pierson, "There was a freshness, vigor, and terseness in his preaching that gave no indication of failing powers; in fact, he had never seemed more fitted to express and impress the thoughts of God."

When he was younger, George was often ill, but as he grew older, he seemed to outgrow his infirmities. In 1837 he feared he would go insane, so great was the pressure in his head, and often his stomach gave him severe trouble. On his ninetieth birthday, when he spoke to the Bethesda congregation, he remarked that his voice and chest were stronger than when he commenced preaching sixty-nine years earlier. By the time he was ninety-two, he wrote, "I have been able every day, and all the day, to work, and that with ease as seventy years since."

Someone observing him noted, "His mental powers too were as clear as when he passed his examinations. For sixty-nine years and ten months he had been a happy man. That he attributed to two things. First, he had maintained a good conscience, not willfully going on a course he knew to be contrary to the mind of God. Secondly, to his love of the Holy Scriptures."

George loved the Scriptures more at ninety than at thirty. This desire grew upon him with age. In his reading, he found his greatest pleasure, and every day he waited for the Lord to speak to him through His Word.

During his final years, George continued to get up at an

early hour, spending several hours reading the Bible. At eight, he went through his correspondence. Following these activities, he met with his assistants and laid out much of their work.

A reporter from the Christian Commonwealth who visited George in 1892 said, "I was prepared to see a venerable-looking gentleman, bent beneath the weight of years, and physically feeble. To my surprise, I found Mr. Müller in appearance a man of considerable bodily vigor. His tall, stately form was, as far as I observed, not in the least bowed by age, and when he afterwards accompanied me along the corridor his step was firm and his stride lengthy and rapid."

The reporter continued: "His face wears an expression of austerity, and his strongly marked features show that he is a man of iron. Yet he knows how to smile, and when he does this, you see quite another aspect of his nature. His manners are those of a prince. He speaks with great deliberation, with a noticeable German accent. Here is a man eighty-seven years of age still carrying on with his own hand certainly one of the most remarkable organizations in the history of the world. An idea of the extent of his work may be gathered from the fact that he has, so he told me, seven assistants for correspondence alone."

On January 13, 1895, George's wife, Susannah, died. While he missed her, he stayed very busy, and seemingly had no time for loneliness. As he had for his first wife, George preached Susannah's funeral sermon. As one of the funeral attendees noted: "I had an opportunity on last Friday of attending the funeral services of Mrs. Müller and witnessing a simple ceremony, perhaps unique in the history of the world.

Here the venerable and venerated patriarch conducted the whole service, and at the age of ninety seemed full of grand faith which has enabled him to accomplish so much and support him in all vicissitudes, trials and labors of a long life."

Two years later, in the summer of 1897, the heat was intense in Bristol, and George experience a brief illness from which he soon recovered. He went about his normal duties for a short time. He began to do all the activities he had been involved in: preaching each Sunday, attending prayer meetings, and helping Mr. Wright oversee the needs of the home.

On the Sunday morning prior to his death, he preached at the Alma Road Chapel. Then in the evening, he preached at his beloved home church, Bethesda Chapel, where he had ministered for sixty-six years. He chose as his text 2 Corinthians 5:1: "For we know that if our earthly house of this tabernacle were dissolved, we have a building of God, an house not made with hands, eternal in the heavens." When George preached that evening, a quiet graciousness seemed to come on the service, and the Lord's presence was felt by the congregation.

But on Wednesday, March 9, 1898, George admitted to his son-in-law that he felt a certain weakness and had to rest several times while dressing. An hour or so later, he told Mr. Wright that "the weakness has passed away; I feel quite myself again." Despite Mr. Wright's suggestion to not work so hard that day, George took part in his regular activities and answered correspondence.

The following morning, March 10, a servant went to George's room with a cup of tea, as was his custom. When no one responded to his knock, he opened the door and found George lying on the floor. When the doctor was summoned, he thought he had probably been dead an hour or so. A friend learning of his death remarked, "Dear old Mr. Müller. He just slipped quietly off home as the gentle Master opened the door and whispered, 'Come.'"

George Müller's death, even at the old age of ninety-three, touched people all over the world. The golden chain of prayer that George's life of trust had woven finally broke. In his lifetime, he estimated God had answered over fifty thousand of his prayers, many thousands of which were answered on the day he made them and often before he arose from his knees.

His funeral took place at the third orphan house on Monday, March 14. Many people, including over a thousand children, attended. After the brief service, the crowd made their way to the Arno Vale Cemetery.

George's body was buried beside his two wives in an ordinary grave. It stands on the slope of a hill under the shade of a yew tree. The coffin displayed simple markings: "George Müller, fell asleep 10th March, 1898, in his 93rd year."

Although many monetary gifts poured in and there was talk of an expensive monument, Mr. Wright could not agree to it. Instead, a simple marker noted the final resting place of this giant of the faith.

George's monument could not be in marble because it had already been erected in the hearts of loving followers. Many of these had preceded him to heaven—the thousands of orphans he had fed and clothed, the multitudes who had been taught in Sunday schools due to his prayer diligence, those brought to the Savior on mission fields through workers who had been supported by his prayer generosity, and the millions who had read the Scriptures and tracts which his faith provided.

Thus George Müller's long life of dedicated service came to a close. But for years to come the example set by God's dedicated servant has spoken to countless people all over the world. Truly it can be said of him: "He being dead, yet speaketh" (Hebrews 11:4).

his legacy

When George Muller died in 1898 his life's work came to an end. For nearly seventy years, a prayer had accompanied nearly every breath he took. Those prayers formed the foundation for the orphanage and the work of the Institution. The question remains: "What lasting effect could such an exemplary life have?" Although it is not possible to take actual measurements of the effects of his life, the work he started has continued—especially in the hearts and minds of those who knew him or had heard of him.

Since there was no financial legacy left at the time of his death, the prayers George had prayed for years continued to yield results. In fact, nine days before his death, after a period of time without any gifts, God suddenly opened the flood gates of blessings and sent in 1,427 pounds. These blessings proved to be the "first fruits" of George's amazing legacy.

Again, responding to his unanswered petitions, the Lord graciously provided thousands of pounds in donations within the next few months following his death. Then, in answer to prayer, God raised up a co-worker for James Wright—someone to share the heavy responsibilities of the orphanage and the Institution.

The year after George's death, the income totalled 29,670 pounds; and the following year, it grew to 43,985 pounds, which showed God's continued blessing on the work and its administrators. During the years from 1900 to 1904, there was always a substantial balance on hand, and at one time this balance amounted to more than $57,000.

Through the years—even up to the time of World War II —the work of the orphanage and the Institution has enjoyed the blessings of God. The latest Institution Report in 1939 revealed a total income for the Orphanage fund of 34,322 pounds, 8s., 9d. The Report also showed a balance on hand of 7 pounds, 124s., 91/2d. The Report's conclusion emphasizes the work's prosperous state: *"Without anyone having been personally applied to by us for a donation,* 2,369,747 pounds, 12s., 8 3/4d., has been received for the Orphans, *as a result of prayer to God,* since the commencement of the work, which sum included the amount received for the Building Fund for the five Houses. Besides this, articles of clothing, furniture, and of food have been given in great variety for the use of the Orphans."

Some critics said that when George Muller died his work on earth would dwindle and finally die. But as long as faith remains the work will continue, and prove again what George always maintained that *the living God is living still,* His shadow stretches into the future, and the work he founded continues to carry the gospel truth to the ends of the earth. Though he is present with the Lord his influence remains and increases with each passing day. The results can be safely left with the Lord. As George once said, "The Lord himself will be the Judge of whatever has been accomplished here on earth."

HEROES OF THE FAITH

This exciting biographical series explores the lives of famous Christian men and women throughout the ages. These trade paper books will inspire and encourage you to follow the example of these "Heroes of the Faith" who made Christ the center of their existence. 208 pages each. Only $3.97 each!

John Bunyan,
Author of The Pilgrim's Progress
Sam Wellman
·
William Carey,
Father of Missions
Sam Wellman
·
Fanny Crosby, the Hymn Writer
Bernard Ruffin
·
Jim Elliot, Missionary to Ecuador
Susan Miller
·
Billy Graham, the Great Evangelist
Sam Wellman
·
C.S. Lewis,
Author of Mere Christianity
Sam Wellman
·
David Livingstone,
Missionary and Explorer
Sam Wellman
·
Martin Luther, the Great Reformer
Dan Harmon
·
D.L. Moody,
the American Evangelist
Bonnie Harvey

Samuel Morris,
the Apostle of Simple Faith
W. Terry Whalin
·
Mother Teresa,
Missionary of Charity
Sam Wellman
·
John Newton,
Author of "Amazing Grace"
Anne Sandberg
·
Charles Spurgeon,
the Great Orator
Dan Harmon
·
Corrie ten Boom,
Heroine of Haarlem
Sam Wellman
·
Sojourner Truth,
American Abolitionist
W. Terry Whalin
·
John Wesley, the Great Methodist
Sam Wellman